Prompt Engineering Guide

"Mastering AI Dialogue for Beginners"

Derek Brooks

Table of Contents

Introduction 4

Chapter One: Basics of Conversational AI 14

Chapter Two: Dive into Prompt Engineering.........................24

Chapter Three: Foundations of Crafting Prompts 32

Chapter Four: Strategies for Effective Prompts 40

Chapter Five: Evaluating and Testing Prompts 49

Chapter Six: Advanced Prompt Techniques..........................58

Chapter Seven: Overcoming Challenges in Prompt Engineering...68

Chapter Eight: Tools and Technologies for Prompt Engineering...77

Chapter Nine: Ethical Considerations in Prompt Design 86

Chapter Ten: Case Studies in Effective Prompt Engineering 96

Chapter Eleven: The Future of Prompt Engineering 107

Chapter Twelve: Building a Career in Prompt Engineering...117

Chapter Thirteen: Community and Further Resources 129

Conclusion..139

Introduction

The importance of prompt engineering in AI dialogue systems

In the rapidly evolving world of technological advancements, dialogue systems have emerged as a critical juncture between human-computer interaction and machine learning methodologies. These systems aim to emulate human conversations, striving to offer users engagements that feel as close to genuine human exchanges as possible. A pivotal factor in achieving this goal is the meticulous practice of prompt engineering in AI dialogue systems.

Essentially, a prompt acts as an instruction or query presented to an AI model, guiding its subsequent output. To draw an analogy, it's similar to framing a question in a particular manner to elicit a desired response. As AI models, especially the likes of transformer-based models such as GPT-3 and BERT, have increased in sophistication, the craft of creating accurate and effective prompts has become increasingly vital. The efficacy of a prompt can significantly influence whether the AI delivers a pertinent, logical reply or an answer that diverges from the user's expectations.

A central rationale behind the significance of prompt engineering lies in the foundational workings of machine learning models. Most modern AI dialogue systems are structured on extensive datasets and function by predicting subsequent words in a sequence based on a probability model.

These systems, devoid of human comprehension, generate replies based on patterns detected during training. Hence, the specific wording, arrangement, and context of a prompt can heavily sway the model's output.

Consider, for example, the dilemma posed by ambiguous queries. An input such as "How tall is he?" presents multiple response avenues for the AI, ranging from data about a previously referenced individual to general statements on human height averages. Through prompt engineering, AI systems are steered towards producing outputs that align more seamlessly with the user's implied context or intended question, thus enhancing the relevance of the response.

Furthermore, considering that AI models are often molded by vast and varied data collections, there's a potential for them to produce biased, inappropriate, or even incorrect outputs. Here, prompt engineering steps in as a safeguard. By meticulously crafting prompts, we can reduce the risks associated with AI models offering skewed, offensive, or erroneous information, ensuring interactions remain ethical, safeguard user data, and meet set content standards.

On the experiential front, prompt engineering significantly elevates user interaction quality. True human interaction isn't merely an exchange of data but a complex dance of emotions, contexts, and subtexts. Through adept prompt design, AI systems can be guided to produce outputs that are not just accurate but also emotionally tuned, context-aware, and, when suitable, light-hearted.

When we zoom out and analyze overarching user engagement patterns, the aggregated benefits of prompt engineering become strikingly evident. Dialogue systems underpinned by sophisticated prompt engineering typically showcase improved user satisfaction metrics, extended interaction durations, and heightened repeat user rates. Such parameters are indispensable for enterprises harnessing AI for tasks like customer assistance, content creation, or interactive digital platforms.

Technically, prompt engineering extends beyond the mere act of crafting effective questions. It embodies an iterative, feedback-driven cycle necessitating continuous refinement. As AI models interact with users, these interactions' feedback can be harnessed to recalibrate and optimize prompts. Advanced tactics, like contrasting different prompts intended for similar outputs, can offer insights into optimal phrasings and structures.

In summation, as technological integration intensifies in our daily experiences, the nuances of human-machine interactions gain paramount importance. At the core of this interplay, particularly in dialogue systems, lies the intricate practice of prompt engineering. It plays an instrumental role in guiding AI interactions, ensuring ethical standards, amplifying user experience, and fostering engagement, making it an integral facet in our quest to harmonize technological and human exchanges. It isn't merely about facilitating AI communication; it's about refining AI interactions to resonate deeply and authentically with the human experience.

Overview of the book structure and what readers can expect

Navigating the vast landscape of contemporary literature requires a clear understanding of a book's organization and offerings. This article endeavors to demystify the structural essence of the book and set forth a transparent guide of its content, ensuring readers can confidently engage with the material.

Underpinning and Composition

Every esteemed book follows a logical sequence of ideas, escorting the reader from basic familiarization to sophisticated comprehension of the topic. Our book closely adheres to this principle. Through a meticulously curated sequence, it facilitates smooth transitions between sections, challenging the reader's intellect while preventing cognitive overwhelm.

Introduction: Setting the Stage

The initial segment is a pivotal one. It not only resonates with the overall tenor of the work but also affords readers an insight into the pivotal themes awaiting exploration. By outlining the broader context and offering a snapshot of the book's objectives, the introduction functions as a preparatory stage, laying out a clear path for the reader to follow.

Principal Sections: The Epicenter of Knowledge

The main body encapsulates the lion's share of the material. Strategically segmented, each part concentrates on a particular facet, ensuring clarity and depth. Here's a breakdown:

Basic Constructs: The preliminary sections prioritize essential principles. By introducing and elaborating on these core tenets, the book equips readers with the requisite knowledge base, preparing them for more intricate analyses in the succeeding chapters.

Real-world Illustrations and Utility: Theory without practice remains abstract. To bridge this gap, certain chapters present tangible examples and real-life cases, illustrating the relevance and applicability of the discussed concepts.

Sophisticated Discussions: Having established a sturdy foundational knowledge, the narrative then ventures into deeper waters, dissecting advanced ideas and challenging conventional wisdom.

Participatory Elements: To foster active engagement, certain sections incorporate interactive modules, ranging from cognitive challenges to reflective tasks. Such components propel readers from passive absorption to active application.

Graphical Enhancements: Aiding Perception

To balance the textual content and amplify understanding, the book is interspersed with visual cues, diagrams, and illustrative aids. Far from ornamental, these visuals simplify intricate notions, offer lucid representations, and provide a refreshing counterpoint to the narrative.

Perspectives from Luminaries: Enriching the Discourse

Interspersed within the content are commentaries, reflections, and opinions from industry stalwarts and subject matter experts. These nuggets enrich the discourse, corroborating assertions, and offering readers a panoramic view of the subject's landscape.

Epilogue: Weaving the Threads

As readers approach the book's conclusion, the epilogue serves to amalgamate the diverse topics and discussions, presenting a coherent and concise recap. It reinforces key concepts, solidifying the reader's grasp of the material.

Supplementary Content and Additional Readings: Extending the Horizon

For the insatiably curious, the book culminates with a supplementary section, detailing additional resources, readings, and platforms. This reservoir of knowledge encourages readers to extend their exploration, delving deeper into the realm of the subject.

To conclude, this book has been fashioned with meticulous care, keeping the reader's experience at its core. It aspires to be more than a trove of information; it seeks to mentor, guide, and accompany the reader through a scholarly expedition. Whether you're at the outset of your intellectual journey or further along, this book assures a systematic, profound, and enlightening engagement. Prepare for an expedition of knowledge, revelation, and deep intellectual enrichment.

Brief touch on the evolution of conversational AI

The progression of conversational AI offers a compelling narrative on the intertwining of human communication intricacies with computational advancements. A look back at its developmental pathway illuminates its transformative journey.

Beginnings: Scripted Interactions

The embryonic stages of conversational AI are rooted in the early endeavors of computer scientists aiming to recreate human dialogues. One of the seminal prototypes, ELIZA, birthed in the MIT Artificial Intelligence Laboratory by Joseph Weizenbaum in the 1960s, stood as a beacon of early achievements. Operating as a basic chatbot, ELIZA utilized straightforward pattern-recognition techniques to mimic the interaction style of a psychotherapist. While groundbreaking, its deterministic, script-based responses underscored the nascent state of the technology.

Yet, the primary drawback of such systems was evident: they were rigidly anchored to their pre-established rules, lacking the agility to navigate conversations beyond their preordained scripts. This underscored the imperative for more versatile, learning-centric approaches.

The Shift Toward Machine Learning

The incorporation of machine learning (ML) techniques into conversational designs heralded a marked evolution. Moving away from static rules, these systems started harnessing data-driven insights, refining their interactions based on accumulated knowledge. Over iterative training cycles, these ML-equipped systems could discern linguistic patterns, ascertain user intentions, and sculpt responses, offering a degree of flexibility hitherto unseen.

One such iteration, ALICE (Artificial Linguistic Internet Computer Entity), developed in the late 20th century, symbolized this transitional phase. With heuristic algorithms driving its interactions, ALICE showcased a more refined, albeit constrained, conversational capability compared to its forerunners.

Deep Learning and the Emergence of Transformers

The leap into deep learning, particularly in the 2010s, signified another pivotal moment. Specialized neural structures, notably recurrent neural networks (RNNs) and their evolved counterparts, long short-term memory (LSTM) networks, emerged as ideal candidates for processing language sequences.

Yet, the transformation was supercharged with the advent of transformer-based architectures. Solutions like Google's BERT (Bidirectional Encoder Representations from Transformers) and OpenAI's GPT (Generative Pre-trained Transformer) employed these novel structures, focusing on self-attention dynamics. This allowed for a more nuanced interpretation of sentence structures, ensuring superior contextual understanding and articulation. Their expansive training capacities further propelled conversational AI into new frontiers of efficiency.

The Rise of Multifaceted Communication Systems

As the domain evolved, the focus expanded from text-centric interactions to encapsulate a broader spectrum of communication channels. Modern systems began to assimilate voice, visual inputs, and even gesture-based cues, aiming for a richer, more holistic interaction palette.

Voice-activated virtual assistants, exemplified by the likes of Siri, Google Assistant, and Alexa, became the flag bearers of this paradigm. Their capability to process spoken language, interpret it, and render coherent responses showcased the maturation of voice-centric conversational AI.

Navigating Conversations with Ethical and Contextual Acuity

With the technical capabilities of conversational AI seeing rapid maturation, there's been a parallel emphasis on refining their ethical compass and contextual discernment. The present trajectory seeks to mold models that engage not just with computational precision but with cultural, societal, and individual awareness. Efforts are concentrated on reducing inherent biases, ensuring information accuracy, and crafting interactions that exude empathy and cognizance.

In Summation

Tracing the metamorphosis of conversational AI, from rudimentary, script-based dialogues to today's multifaceted, contextually aware systems, paints a picture of relentless innovation. As we teeter on the brink of further advancements, conversational AI promises to continually reshape our digital communication frameworks, highlighting the harmonious synergy between human and technological capabilities.

Chapter One

Basics of Conversational AI

Understanding dialogue systems

Dialogue systems, in the realm of digital advancements, have become essential instruments in fostering enriched human-computer relationships. As tools tailored to simulate human conversations, they're ushering in an era of more direct and adaptive exchanges between individuals and digital entities. A closer exploration into their complexities unveils a world of opportunities and applications.

Essentially, dialogue systems are structured to comprehend, decode, and reply to user statements, ensuring fluid conversational transitions. Their operational success is anchored in their multifaceted infrastructure, optimized algorithms, and deep-rooted understanding of language intricacies. Their evolution is a blend of technological innovation and strides in the fields of cognitive and computational linguistics.

Classifying Dialogue Systems

Conventionally, dialogue systems fall into two distinct types:

Goal-Oriented Systems: As the name suggests, these are built with a particular purpose or function in mind, such as scheduling appointments, addressing queries, or setting alarms. Their primary focus remains on driving specific outcomes, with a more restricted but efficient knowledge base.

General Conversation Systems: These variants, commonly known as chatbots, are geared for more informal, expansive conversations without a predetermined goal. They're equipped with extensive knowledge repositories and are tuned for engaging dialogues across various subjects.

Operational Dynamics

The functional core of dialogue systems draws heavily from the principles of natural language processing (NLP). Delving into the basics:

Decoding the User's Input: The initial task revolves around dissecting and understanding the user's message. This includes segmenting sentences, grasping language constructs, and pinpointing the underlying intention of the user.

Crafting a Reply: Armed with this insight, the system then molds a fitting response. This could involve retrieving information, analyzing the query, or utilizing trained models to construct answers.

Delivering the Answer: The last step entails presenting the curated reply to the user in a clear and engaging manner.

These systems' efficiency is founded on models that have been honed on extensive data troves, granting them the capability to gauge context, identify linguistic trends, and tailor responses that resonate with the user's intent.

From Conventional Methods to Neural Frameworks

In earlier times, dialogue systems predominantly operated on set rules, steered by predefined frameworks shaped by human experts. Decision-making trees and handcrafted databases were the norm. However, the embrace of deep learning and the emergence of neural networks have revolutionized their design and function.

Today's systems often employ structures like Recurrent Neural Networks (RNNs), Long Short-Term Memory (LSTM) cells, and the avant-garde transformer models. When educated on vast conversational datasets, these models can predict and tailor more sophisticated and relevant responses without being pre-configured for every conceivable conversation.

Potential Obstacles and the Path Forward

Despite monumental progress, dialogue systems confront several hurdles:

Retaining Context: Sustaining context throughout extended dialogues is a domain ripe for enhancement. Users anticipate systems to recall prior exchanges and factor them into successive interactions.

Deciphering Ambiguities: The fluid nature of human language, with its playfulness and nuances, poses challenges. Systems must be adept at navigating linguistic ambiguities, cultural references, and even humor.

Ethical Dimensions: As with evolving digital technologies, there's an onus to ensure that dialogue systems function ethically, transparently, and devoid of prejudices.

Anticipating the future, with AI and NLP maturing, dialogue systems are set to achieve unparalleled finesse. Potential integrations with immersive platforms like augmented reality (AR) and virtual reality (VR), diverse input methods, and instantaneous language translation suggest a promising trajectory, edging closer to natural human dialogues.

To sum up, grasping the essence of dialogue systems offers insights into the thrilling fusion of language studies, cognitive research, and technological prowess. These evolving tools, with their expanding capabilities, promise a future where our digital dialogues rival the depth and spontaneity of human interactions.

Different types of chatbots: Rule-based vs AI-driven

In today's fast-paced digital milieu, chatbots stand as pivotal tools that streamline user engagement and modernize business processes. Acting as automated conversational agents, chatbots have found their niche across numerous platforms, from support channels to interactive websites. The genesis and growth of chatbots can be traced to two primary philosophies: deterministic rule-bound systems and those propelled by artificial intelligence. Distinguishing between these philosophies offers a deep dive into their unique merits, constraints, and optimal utilization scenarios.

Rule-based Chatbots

These chatbots, grounded in fixed algorithms and logical branches, are the foundational pillars in automated conversation. Operating within a clear-cut framework, they render responses based on explicit criteria outlined by developers.

Framework and Functionality: Rule-based chatbots are built around the "cause-and-effect" principle. When they receive a user's inquiry, they reference a predefined set of criteria to produce the most fitting response. It's similar to traversing a decision map where each user's input corresponds to a designated pathway and output.

Advantages:

Consistent Outputs. With rule based models, the outcomes are stable and dependable. A particular user input always triggers a known response.

Straightforward Development: For tasks with limited scope or clear objectives, rule-based chatbots offer a quick deployment cycle.

Defined Operational Limits: Their operation is bound by clear constraints, ensuring they don't deviate into unpredictable territory.

Drawbacks:

Inflexibility: These chatbots falter when presented with inputs that deviate from their rulebook.

Complexity with Expansion: As the spectrum of user questions grows, the logical branches become increasingly intricate.

Static Behavior: They lack the ability to assimilate new information or evolve with changing user patterns.

AI-driven Chatbots

These chatbots harness the capabilities of artificial intelligence, especially the tenets of natural language processing (NLP) and machine learning. Their hallmark is their adaptability and their capacity to refine themselves over time.

Framework and Functionality: Rooted in extensive data libraries and advanced algorithms, AI-driven chatbots process user input, discern its intent, and craft a response. With every new user interaction, they recalibrate their mechanisms, striving for improved accuracy and relevance.

Advantages:

Dynamic Response Mechanism: They can adeptly handle a broad spectrum of inquiries, even those they haven't been specifically tailored for.

Evolutionary Design: With machine learning at their core, these chatbots enhance their performance iteratively.

Understanding Nuances: Their robust NLP capacities enable them to perceive context, emotional undertones, and intricate linguistic subtleties.

Drawbacks:

Challenging Deployment: Setting up a proficient AI-driven chatbot necessitates deep knowledge in fields like machine learning and NLP.

Reliance on Data: Their performance is tied to the quality and expanse of training datasets.

Response Variability: Without hard-coded responses, there exists a minor possibility of generating unintended outputs.

Final Reflections

Although the distinction between rule-based and AI-driven chatbots is evident, the decision to adopt one isn't straightforward. It pivots on precise needs, budgetary considerations, and the envisioned application spectrum. Rule-based chatbots, in their defined realm, excel in scenarios where user interactions are predictable and narrow. Conversely, AI-driven chatbots emerge as victors in settings demanding versatility and continuous adaptation.

With chatbot technologies witnessing continuous innovation, amalgamated models, blending the steadfastness of deterministic systems with the agility of AI-propelled frameworks, are gaining momentum. Such synergistic models pave the way for conversational agents that combine reliability, adaptability, and evolutionary prowess, marking a significant leap in user engagement paradigms.

Role of natural language processing (NLP)

Natural Language Processing (NLP) stands as a remarkable fusion of artificial intelligence (AI) and linguistics, aiming to bridge the gap between human communication nuances and computational understanding. The evolution of NLP is nothing short of astounding. From its early days of basic rule-driven approaches, NLP has transitioned into a domain dominated by advanced techniques like deep learning and neural architectures.

A quintessential application of NLP is evident in information retrieval systems. Every query entered into a search engine, with the expectation of a precise response, leans on NLP's strength. These systems navigate vast datasets, discerning user intent and contextual nuances, to deliver highly relevant results. This capability has been enhanced by the evolution of semantic search, focusing on understanding content essence rather than mere keyword matching.

Moreover, NLP's potential shines in sentiment analysis, a crucial tool for modern businesses. This process enables firms to discern public emotions and perceptions related to their offerings by evaluating diverse content, from social media chatter to elaborate customer feedback. By deciphering the underlying emotion in textual fragments, businesses can derive actionable insights into market reception and customer preferences.

Content summarization is another domain where NLP's efficiency is clearly visible. Given the vast swathes of information available online, there's an ever-growing demand for brief, yet comprehensive content summaries. NLP algorithms are adept at analyzing extensive documents and producing condensed versions without compromising the core message. This is immensely beneficial for professionals in research, media, and legal sectors who often need to quickly understand lengthy documents.

Furthermore, machine translation has witnessed remarkable improvements courtesy of NLP. Contemporary translation tools, enriched by sophisticated NLP algorithms, offer translations that respect not just literal semantics but also cultural and idiomatic nuances, facilitating more genuine and meaningful cross-linguistic interactions.

In the realm of creative content generation, NLP is blurring boundaries. From crafting compelling marketing narratives to generating news briefs, advanced NLP algorithms challenge the conventional belief of creativity being solely a human attribute. By recognizing and imitating stylistic patterns, these systems can produce content that genuinely resonates with its audience.

Yet, one of the most commendable contributions of NLP is its role in making digital content more inclusive. Voice-driven interfaces, enhanced by NLP, are opening up digital avenues for individuals with visual or reading challenges. Simultaneously, real-time transcription services, powered by NLP, are ensuring auditory content is accessible to those with hearing limitations.

However, the evolution of NLP is not without its set of challenges. Deep learning-driven NLP models demand extensive, high-quality training datasets. The efficacy and neutrality of these models hinge on the quality of this data. If training data lacks diversity or is imbalanced, it could lead to biases. Also, the inherent opacity of deep learning models poses questions about their decision-making processes and overall transparency.

To wrap up, Natural Language Processing's significance in the current tech-driven era is multifaceted and far-reaching. With its continual advancements, championed by innovations in AI and deep learning, NLP is revolutionizing how machines and humans interact. While challenges persist, the myriad benefits, from improved information accessibility to refined human-computer communication, highlight NLP's central role in the digital age.

Chapter Two

Dive into Prompt Engineering

What is prompt engineering?

Within the dynamic landscape of artificial intelligence (AI), prompt engineering stands out as an integral facet, especially as we delve deeper into the intricacies of modern AI systems. To truly grasp the essence of prompt engineering, one must first recognize the complexities of contemporary AI algorithms, notably those that specialize in Natural Language Processing (NLP). Such algorithms, which are predominantly vast neural networks trained on an array of diverse datasets, are meticulously constructed to interpret or produce human-like language. Their ability to generate specific and targeted responses is heavily influenced by the nature and structure of their input. This carefully framed input, often in the form of a question or directive, is termed a 'prompt'. The methodical process of designing these prompts for maximum efficacy is what defines 'prompt engineering'.

From an outsider's perspective, crafting a prompt may seem rather simple. However, the distinction between an adeptly engineered prompt and a rudimentary one can be as vast as the difference between querying a search engine with "latest breakthroughs in biotechnology" versus "science news". The former, due to its precision, is bound to yield richer and more relevant results.

As AI models, particularly those in the linguistic domain, evolve in complexity, the significance of prompt engineering has become increasingly evident. Boasting millions or even billions of parameters, these advanced models hold tremendous potential, but harnessing this potential demands expertise. An artfully designed prompt can steer the model towards generating desired outputs, be it answering intricate questions, creating a narrative, or offering technical recommendations.

So, why does prompt engineering merit such emphasis? A few pivotal reasons include:

Optimal Model Utilization: Despite their sophistication, even top-tier AI models aren't devoid of flaws. They may occasionally produce outputs that veer off-course or lack depth. Ingenious prompts can substantially reduce such discrepancies by offering the model a clearer directive.

Conservation of Resources: Employing complex AI models demands significant computational power. By ensuring the precision of prompts from the get-go, one can cut down on unnecessary computations, thereby optimizing resource usage.

Tailored Results: As AI permeates diverse sectors – from healthcare to banking to creative arts – the demand for industry-specific outputs escalates. Through prompt engineering, inputs can be meticulously crafted to mirror industry-specific standards and expectations.

Boosting Transfer Learning: Transfer learning entails applying knowledge acquired from one domain to enhance performance in a closely related domain. Skillful prompt engineering can smoothen this transition, ensuring knowledge transfer is seamless and effective.

Several techniques can enhance the efficacy of prompt engineering:

Progressive Refinement: Perfecting prompt design often involves a cycle of trial and error. Based on initial outputs, prompts can be progressively fine-tuned to align more closely with desired outcomes.

Feedback Integration: Feedback, whether manually curated or automated, can be invaluable in refining subsequent prompts, ensuring they yield more targeted results.

Incorporating Multiple Modalities: With AI models branching out from textual realms, prompts can be enriched using various mediums, including visuals, auditory cues, or even physical interactions.

Leveraging Domain Insights: Collaborating with industry experts can aid in creating prompts that are in sync with the unique nuances of specialized fields, thereby ensuring model outputs are both relevant and insightful.

To encapsulate, prompt engineering emerges as a crucial discipline, pivotal in maximizing the utility of cutting-edge AI models. As we progress in the AI journey, and as these models burgeon in capabilities, the art of crafting strategic prompts will gain even more prominence. Whether one is a technical expert aiming to tap into the full potential of an AI model or an enterprise keen on leveraging AI for specific applications, an understanding of prompt engineering can be a game-changer.

Importance in current AI dialogue models like GPT series

In today's advanced realm of artificial intelligence, dialogue-driven models have ascended to the forefront, setting new standards and benchmarks. Central to this wave is the GPT (Generative Pre-trained Transformer) lineup, a trailblazer that showcases the depth and breadth of machine understanding of human linguistics. Upon closer examination, one realizes that the stellar performance of models like the GPT isn't just a result of their intricate design, but also hinges significantly on the nuances of their engagement with end-users.

The essence of the GPT models, products of OpenAI's research, revolves around the transformer framework. These models have the notable ability to grasp context, churn out extended, coherent content, and engage users with real-time conversation. While much of this can be credited to their underlying structure, the interaction mechanisms play a pivotal role.

A fundamental characteristic of models like GPT is the absorption and processing of massive data volumes during the training phase. But, in real-world applications, the model necessitates detailed directives to deliver relevant outcomes. This highlights the critical role of prompts and interactional intricacies. A well-framed prompt can channel the model's output in a specific direction, ensuring the optimal utilization of its extensive training.

Equally vital is the feedback mechanism. Continuous interactions with the model ideally guide its evolution, honing its adaptability and alignment with dynamic user needs. This adaptability is essential to retain the model's relevance in an ever-evolving technological environment.

The GPT models are finding roles in varied spheres, from digital assistance to creative content development. Every application domain brings its set of challenges and expectations. Ensuring the GPT model meets these specific demands is not just about the underlying technology but significantly involves refining the engagement methodologies and the quality of inputs.

However, it's crucial to recognize that even advanced systems like the GPT series have limitations. There can be occasions when the outputs aren't entirely accurate or context-appropriate. These challenges point towards the need to enhance not only the model's core design but also the interaction framework. Ensuring clarity and contextual richness in prompts can help minimize misaligned responses.

Addressing the critical topic of ethical considerations, AI models mirror the biases in their training datasets. If unchecked, the model's responses might unintentionally echo these biases. Navigating this requires multiple interventions, from refining data sources, adjusting model architecture, and importantly, evolving interaction methods that can recognize and counteract potential biases. This aspect is becoming increasingly pivotal in our collective pursuit of responsible AI.

To summarize, while the advanced design of AI dialogue models, epitomized by the GPT series, forms their backbone, the interactive elements that bring these models to life are equally significant. Whether through refined prompts, continuous feedback, tailored engagements, or ethical considerations, the delicate dance between technological intricacy and human engagement will define the trajectory of AI's continuing evolution.

The intersection of linguistics, psychology, and technology

As we advance into a digitally-driven era, the melding of linguistics, psychology, and technology unveils a new horizon in the exploration of human cognition, communication, and technological innovation. This blend unveils the profound depths of human thought processes and their linguistic expressions, while also presenting opportunities to leverage these insights in technological domains.

Linguistics delves deep into the intricacies of language—encompassing its form, development, variations, and most importantly, its pivotal role in human interaction and self-expression. Beyond being a mere set of symbols and syntactical rules, language is a mirror to cultural imprints, historical evolutions, and the rich tapestry of human experiences. On the other hand, psychology offers a window into the cognitive undercurrents governing language assimilation, interpretation, and articulation.

Through the prism of psychology, we gain insights into human information processing, the intertwining of emotions with linguistic cues, and the impact of external factors on language-based behaviors. A prominent branch, psycholinguistics, zeroes in on the mental mechanics supporting our ability to understand and produce language. Central to its investigation are themes like childhood language acquisition, bilingual cognitive processing, and the interplay of emotions in shaping language perceptions.

Now, bringing technology into this mix, especially the burgeoning fields of artificial intelligence (AI) and machine learning, adds another layer of depth. The objective here is to replicate or even enhance human cognitive functionalities using computational algorithms. The aspiration to birth machines capable of comprehending and crafting human-like linguistic outputs has fueled research that sits at the nexus of linguistics and technological advancements. This is where Natural Language Processing (NLP) finds its footing, leveraging linguistic tenets to decipher and formulate human language.

However, to architect technological tools that capture the essence of human language, a mere structural understanding won't suffice. It's imperative to factor in the psychological facets—delving into human thought patterns, perceptions, and linguistic processing mechanisms. This is evident in contemporary tools for sentiment analysis and advanced conversational AI platforms. Such tools go beyond parsing linguistic constructs; they aim to discern underlying intents, sentiments, and emotional hues, drawing deeply from psychological doctrines.

Consider advanced conversational platforms: their design ethos revolves around not just linguistically processing user inputs but also detecting underlying emotional states. Responses are sculpted in alignment with inferred emotions, marking a paradigm shift from basic rule-driven platforms to sophisticated, contextually aware systems.

Furthermore, modern language translators serve as another testament. Earlier versions, while technically correct, often missed the mark on capturing cultural or contextual subtleties, yielding results that felt inauthentic. Contemporary models, enriched by linguistic and psychological insights, endeavor to produce translations that resonate with both literal and contextual semantics.

Nevertheless, weaving linguistics, psychology, and technology presents its share of challenges. The sheer diversity and depth of human languages, intertwined with complex cognitive networks, set a high benchmark. Moreover, while data-centric technology vies for universal applicability, languages are deeply personal, regional, and cultural. Reconciling technological efficiency with the multifaceted landscape of human language is a continuous journey.

To wrap up, the symbiosis of linguistics, psychology, and technology heralds a captivating juncture in our journey to decode human cognitive processes and communication paradigms. As AI's evolution accelerates, its fusion with linguistics and psychology will deepen, giving rise to innovations echoing the genuine human linguistic experience. Embedded in this synergy is the vision of creating machines that resonate authentically and dynamically with the multifarious hues of human communication.

Chapter Three

Foundations of Crafting Prompts

Understanding user intent

In today's digital landscape, one of the foremost considerations for developers, designers, and businesses is to accurately interpret user intent. It goes beyond the surface-level actions or words of users; it delves into the heart of what they genuinely aim to achieve. By effectively decoding user intent, organizations can elevate user experiences, fine-tune their digital platforms, and provide unparalleled value.

User intent can be defined as the specific purpose or goal underlying a user's interaction with a digital entity, such as a website, application, chatbot, or search engine. This interaction might manifest as a typed search query, a product click, or a webpage navigation. Traditionally, digital systems heavily relied on these overt actions or inputs to infer a user's behavior. However, these explicit signals often gave a somewhat narrow view, missing the broader contextual factors that provide depth to a user's intent.

As technological advancements have made their mark, especially with the rise of artificial intelligence (AI) and machine learning (ML), our capability to decode user intent has undergone a transformation. The major transition has been from a straightforward approach, which directly associates actions to intents, to one that encompasses context and multiple other influencing factors. For example, a user searching for "beach attire" during winter might be prepping for a vacation rather than making an off-season purchase. Here, contextual understanding combined with historical data can shed light on the true intent behind such a search.

The strides made in Natural Language Processing (NLP) significantly contribute to enhancing this understanding. NLP enables machines to process and interpret human language, ensuring they don't just focus on words but also on sentiment, nuance, and the broader purpose. This becomes especially significant in the domain of voice-activated systems, where user queries are conversational and can carry multiple layers of intent.

The question arises: Why is there such an emphasis on understanding user intent? The crux lies in the potential of curating interactions that resonate with the user. For instance, an online shopping platform can suggest products aligning closely with what the user might be looking for, ensuring satisfaction and potentially boosting sales. Search engines that can pinpoint user intent can provide results that hit the mark, building user trust. For digital assistants, discerning intent accurately is the foundation for delivering apt and meaningful interactions.

Yet, achieving impeccable intent recognition isn't without its complexities. The often elusive nature of human language, with its multiple interpretations based on various factors like context, tone, or cultural background, is a prime challenge. Additionally, as digital solutions cater to a global audience, they encounter a plethora of language styles, idioms, and regional expressions which can influence intent understanding.

Also, it's imperative to understand that while AI and ML have brought about transformative capabilities, they aren't without limitations. Sole dependence on algorithms, without weaving in the human touch of empathy and cultural context, can sometimes miss the mark. Thus, harmonizing technological capabilities with genuine human insight remains the optimal approach.

To sum it up, decoding user intent is both an art and a science. As we continue to integrate sophisticated technological solutions, it's essential to pair them with a profound grasp of human behavior and context. The ultimate aim is to not merely respond to users but to intuitively align with their core desires and needs, paving the way for digital experiences that truly connect, engage, and delight.

Importance of context and history

In the vast expanse of data interpretation, be it human thought processes or digital algorithms, two pillars stand tall: context and history. Their roles are paramount in shaping how we perceive, interpret, and ultimately decide on matters. Absent these two, our judgments could be rooted in partial or misleading data, leading to unsatisfactory results.

Let's delve into context first. At its core, context is the circumstantial frame that surrounds an incident, statement, or idea. It gives texture and layers to narratives, enhancing clarity and comprehension. Take, for instance, the domain of natural language processing (NLP). A term like "bank" can signify a financial entity or a river's edge. Stripped of its context, discerning its correct meaning becomes a convoluted task.

Moreover, context acts as a bridge in communication, sprinkling nuances that combat the vagueness often associated with language. As artificial intelligence (AI) systems continue to advance, understanding context is becoming indispensable. In platforms like chat interfaces or content recommenders, mere processing of a direct query won't suffice. These platforms need to gauge the surrounding factors, such as previous interactions or the nature of the query, to be genuinely effective.

History offers a different vantage point. Where context provides layers, history gifts us with a broader perspective. It's vital for tracing patterns, tracking changes, and identifying root causes. In fields like data analytics, history comprises the accumulated data over time, nourishing and refining algorithmic outputs.

Consider this analogy: When a patient approaches a doctor with a complaint, the current symptoms serve as the immediate context. But the patient's previous health records, past ailments, and treatments undertaken offer a historical context, enabling a more comprehensive diagnosis. Similarly, in online retail, a shopper's current activity offers a snapshot, but their past interactions and purchases provide a timeline that can be used to tailor recommendations.

Predictive analytics also heavily leans on history. It uses past patterns to predict future behaviors. For instance, while predicting stock market movements, historical market responses to similar past events play a crucial role.

However, seamlessly integrating context and history is not without its challenges. Ensuring the accuracy and relevance of historical data is crucial; outdated or poorly curated data can render insights obsolete. There's also the potential pitfall of placing undue weight on current context, leading to a narrow viewpoint.

Another essential consideration is the ethical dimension of data. As we collect and use more contextual and historical data, we must tread carefully, ensuring we respect individual privacy and avoid any form of bias.

But when harnessed judiciously, the duo of context and history proves powerful. They enrich insights and underpin better decision-making across various sectors, from healthcare to e-commerce. While context offers a snapshot of the present, history provides the chronicle leading up to it. Neglecting one could lead to a fragmented view, but together they offer a comprehensive vista. In today's data-driven age, context and history are not just record-keepers but also the key to unlocking nuanced and actionable insights.

Active listening principles in AI

At the heart of effective communication lies active listening. This vital skill, primarily associated with human interactions, underscores the importance of wholly focusing on the speaker, grasping their conveyed message, and offering insightful feedback. When we adapt these principles to artificial intelligence (AI) systems, the aim extends beyond merely devising intricate algorithms. The objective becomes crafting systems that can foster meaningful user engagements, reminiscent of human dialogues. By embedding active listening tenets into AI, we can significantly elevate user experiences, ensuring they perceive their interactions as validated, comprehensible, and significant.

A pivotal aspect of active listening is undivided attention. In human discourse, this manifests as steady eye contact, gestures of agreement, and refraining from interruptive behaviors. For AI, this requires ensuring that technological platforms are devoid of glitches or delays that might hinder user interactions. Consider a chatbot, for instance. Its design should facilitate smooth handling of various user inputs, eschewing potential system "overloads" or "misinterpretations." It's crucial that the software remains resilient, even amidst dense user traffic, simulating a personal conversation environment for each user.

Understanding, another crucial facet, moves beyond merely decoding words; it's about capturing their essence. Therefore, AI tools need advanced natural language processing (NLP) capabilities, allowing them to not only decipher words' explicit meanings but also to intuit sentiments and intentions. For instance, when a user communicates a statement like, "Today was exhausting," to a digital assistant, the tool should discern the user's mood, perhaps suggesting soothing tunes or relaxation methods. This depth of understanding transcends mere word recognition, entering realms of emotional recognition.

Reacting appropriately to user input is equally critical. Once an AI tool deciphers a user's message, it should reciprocate in a manner that reinforces the user's sentiments or queries. Responses should be prompt, pertinent, and context-sensitive. Suppose a user voices a concern to an AI-fueled customer service agent. In that case, the system should initially validate the expressed issue, subsequently offering resolutions or raising the concern to a higher level if needed. The intent is to establish a reciprocal feedback mechanism, ensuring users witness tangible results from their interactions.

Additionally, recognizing non-verbal signals is essential. While humans effortlessly pick up on these during in-person exchanges, AI encounters unique challenges. Cutting-edge tools, especially those enabled with visual processing features, are evolving to identify facial nuances, posture shifts, and tonal variations. Such capabilities allow AI to holistically evaluate user emotions, fashioning responses based on a blend of spoken and unspoken cues.

One key principle in active listening is eschewing rash conclusions or assumptions. Similarly, AI systems should be programmed to forestall preset reactions based on limited data. Instead, they should gather a comprehensive understanding before formulating any feedback, ensuring thorough user comprehension.

AI's edge over human communicators lies in its access to extensive data repositories. By studying user behavior trends, AI can perpetually refine its listening prowess. Data-driven models can differentiate between responses that resonate with users and those that fall flat, facilitating real-time system enhancements.

However, it's paramount to approach this integration with caution. Overemphasis on AI-driven empathy might seem insincere or unsettling. The endgame isn't necessarily creating human replicas but enhancing user interactions by harnessing human-centric listening techniques. Furthermore, ethical considerations cannot be overstated. Data collection and analysis, aimed at refining AI's listening capabilities, must always prioritize safeguarding user privacy.

In summation, assimilating active listening principles into AI revolves around transcending the transactional boundaries often linked with technological systems. The vision is to fashion tools capable of mirroring the subtleties intrinsic to human exchanges. As AI further infiltrates sectors ranging from wellness to banking, its effectiveness will increasingly be gauged by its adeptness at active listening, a barometer for ensuring users consistently feel acknowledged, comprehended, and cherished.

Chapter Four

Strategies for Effective Prompts

Open-ended vs close-ended prompts

The architecture of digital interactions, particularly those facilitated by AI mechanisms, rests significantly on the type of prompts presented to users. As technology continues its forward march, distinguishing between open-ended and close-ended prompts is essential in refining interaction quality. Both carry inherent attributes and applications, with respective merits and challenges. They guide user feedback and dictate the extent of data engagement.

Close-ended prompts, in essence, seek concise, definitive responses. They often take the form of yes/no questions or multiple-choice options in various platforms. For instance, when a digital tool inquires, "Do you wish to continue?", it anticipates a simple yes or no. These prompts are exceptionally useful when the goal is to obtain clear data, facilitate immediate decisions, or steer a user along a predetermined path. Their directness accelerates operations, removes uncertainties, and empowers systems to quickly organize or act based on received answers.

Such prompts have their niche, especially in situations demanding definitive responses. In time-sensitive scenarios or on platforms with limited display capacity, close-ended questions provide unambiguous directives, mitigating potential user perplexities. In the realm of data interpretation, these prompt responses can be effortlessly compiled, visualized, and assessed, yielding clear insights.

Yet, their concise nature is a double-edged sword. By bounding user feedback, they might overlook deeper insights or sentiments. For example, a user might decline a product's utility, but without added inquiries, the system remains oblivious to the reason or potential enhancements.

On the flip side, open-ended prompts flourish by inviting expansive discussions. Questions such as, "What are your thoughts on our latest offering?" or "Could you elaborate on your interaction with our interface?" beckon users to divulge comprehensive insights or feelings. They shine when the aspiration is in-depth feedback, gauging emotions, or nurturing originality.

For systems powered by AI, open-ended queries are invaluable. The array of user input provides a multi-faceted dataset, permitting algorithms to grasp user nuances more intimately. Such insights pave the way for tailored user engagements, with systems fine-tuning based on comprehensive feedback.

However, the open nature of these prompts carries its own set of challenges. Interpreting wide-ranging responses necessitates sophisticated NLP tools due to the variability in answers. Moreover, while they draw out more detailed information, they might also daunt users or lead to information overload. Absent precise guidelines, some users may meander, delivering prolonged responses that stray from the primary concern.

The decision between using open-ended and close-ended prompts revolves around interaction objectives. For rapid determinations, transparent data, or numerical evaluations, close-ended queries fit the bill. Conversely, when the aim is in-depth insights or gauging complex sentiments, open-ended questions prevail.

To encapsulate, the differentiation between open-ended and close-ended prompts isn't a mere terminological choice but underpins decisions regarding user interaction's depth and nature. As technological advancements shape user platforms, discerning which prompt to deploy will be integral for crafting impactful engagements. A judicious mix, aptly tailored to specific contexts, will unlock the zenith of user-tech dialogues.

Contextual prompts: Using previous dialogue

The evolution of digital communication has ushered in a refined dimension of interaction between humans and computational systems. At the forefront of this dimension is the emergence of contextual prompts, a sophisticated mechanism that capitalizes on preceding conversations to enhance subsequent interactions. These dynamic prompts, distinct from their fixed equivalents, adapt and change based on earlier dialogues, ensuring that ensuing conversations remain pertinent, individualized, and user-oriented.

Tracing Back the Origins

Grasping the relevance of contextual prompts warrants a brief delve into their origins. Early incarnations of automated interactions were mostly static and governed by set rules. Any user query received a preset response, devoid of context or the interaction's historical backdrop. While straightforward, this strategy resulted in fragmented dialogues, rendering the system without a semblance of "recollection" or "cognizance" of earlier exchanges.

Yet, with the rise and refinement of natural language processing (NLP) and machine learning methodologies, the capability to harness, scrutinize, and act on past conversations became increasingly feasible, marking the onset of contextual prompts.

Understanding the Dynamics of Contextual Prompts

At its essence, a contextual prompt hinges on a system's proficiency to recall, discern, and leverage earlier exchanges. Contemporary NLP methodologies can sift through extensive textual data, extracting pivotal topics, intents, and emotions. By archiving these components — either within fleeting session memories or extended user profiles (with explicit user agreement) — the system can hark back to past dialogues when shaping new replies.

For example, should a user initially express interest in vegetarian dishes and later request meal recommendations, a system employing contextual prompts could suggest a vegetarian dish, tying back to the prior conversation.

The Merits of Contextual Prompting

Tailored Interactions: Using past interactions, systems can craft responses that align closely with individual user profiles, thereby heightening user interaction and contentment.

Efficient Exchanges: The use of contextual prompts negates the requirement for users to constantly reiterate information. For instance, once a user's geographical location is known, the system can proffer localized solutions without seeking the same information repeatedly.

Augmented Troubleshooting: For support-related scenarios, grasping a user's historical concerns can lead to more immediate and relevant resolutions. An automated support mechanism can pinpoint repetitive issues, either escalating the concern or offering a more detailed remedy.

Potential Roadblocks and Reflections

Yet, contextual prompting isn't devoid of hurdles. Striking a harmonious balance between bespoke interactions and data privacy remains vital. Users might be apprehensive of platforms that seemingly harbor an excess of personal knowledge. Additionally, ensuring the context's accurate and apt utilization presents a technical challenge. Misguided context usage might lead to irrelevant or incoherent responses.

Furthermore, the duration of retained context becomes a point of deliberation. Some contextual elements might be momentary, while others might have lasting relevance. Determining which fragments of context to preserve and their lifespan becomes an essential task.

Anticipating the Future

The prospects for contextual prompts seem boundless. With the development of decentralized learning techniques, it's conceivable to have systems that assimilate context without centralized data repositories, merging personalization with data protection. As we move towards multi-faceted interfaces (encompassing text, auditory, and visual signals), contextual cues could transcend textual boundaries, paving the path for deeper and more innate interactions.

To encapsulate, by drawing on previous dialogues, contextual prompts signify a pivotal shift in the landscape of human-machine communications. As we navigate this evolving terrain, it's imperative that the quest for personalized interactions remains intertwined with ethical considerations, always aiming to augment and never obstruct the user journey.

Handling ambiguous user queries

In the realm of digital communication interfaces powered by artificial intelligence and natural language processing, ambiguity stands as a persistent hurdle. The multifaceted nuances of human language present scenarios where a single input may possess multiple valid interpretations. To navigate this intricacy, a fusion of linguistic insights, cutting-edge technology, and user-oriented design is imperative.

The Nature of Ambiguity

Ambiguous queries are those where a distinct interpretation is elusive due to the inherent multiplicity of meanings. Consider the inquiry, "How's the apple?". In the absence of context, one might wonder if it pertains to the fruit's taste, a tech product's performance, or even an artistic depiction. Ambiguity typically emanates from three primary sources: word-level ambiguities, structural ambiguities, and meaning-driven ambiguities.

Unraveling Ambiguity's Roots

Words with Dual Meanings: Certain terms, like "bark" (of a tree or a dog's sound), can introduce word-based ambiguities due to their multiple inherent meanings.

Sentence Construction: Ambiguity can arise from how sentences are framed. "She met her father wearing a hat" could signify either the father or the daughter wearing the hat, depending on the reader's interpretation.

Lacking Clear References: Phrases or pronouns without an immediately identifiable reference can pose challenges. For instance, "Anna told Sarah she was late" leaves one wondering who exactly was late.

Strategies to Navigate Ambiguity

Evaluating Context: Many modern virtual assistants and chatbots utilize context to deduce the meaning behind ambiguous phrases. Extracting insights from preceding interactions aids these platforms in accurately gauging user intent.

Statistical Approaches: Methods rooted in statistics, such as Bayesian models, can assist in predicting a user's intended meaning based on accumulated data and pattern recognition.

Seeking Clarification: When in doubt, systems might directly engage the user to clarify their query. Rather than making an uninformed guess, this direct approach often proves more efficient and user-friendly.

Conceptual Linkages: By associating ambiguous terms with specific, known concepts via tools like knowledge graphs, systems can considerably narrow down potential meanings.

Analyzing User Behavior Patterns: Sometimes, ancillary cues like the user's typing speed, choice of terms, or even metadata such as their geolocation, can provide valuable hints about their intended meaning.

Challenges on the Horizon

Despite the vast strides made in ambiguity resolution, the path is strewn with complexities. The dynamism of human language, colored by regional dialects and personal quirks, defies any universally applicable solution. Additionally, while data-driven insights are invaluable, over-dependence can sometimes skew interpretations unduly in favor of past patterns.

Equally critical is maintaining a harmonious equilibrium between automated decision-making and seeking user input. An overzealous system that frequently interrupts for clarifications can be as problematic as one that consistently misinterprets user queries.

The Journey Forward

The ongoing advancements in natural language processing technologies offer hope. The infusion of deep learning, broader training data sets, and enhanced algorithms for context comprehension suggests a future where ambiguous queries are addressed even more effectively.

Moreover, as interfaces grow more adept at natural language interpretation, they'll also become better at signaling areas of uncertainty, leading to a more collaborative and seamless user experience.

To wrap up, while ambiguous user queries remain a challenging aspect of digital communication, they also drive innovations in technology, pushing the boundaries of what's possible and charting the path for more intuitive and intelligent interactive platforms.

Chapter Five

Evaluating and Testing Prompts

The feedback loop: iterative refinement

The cyclical process of iterative refinement, underpinned by feedback loops, is pivotal in ensuring systems and methodologies evolve and mature. Whether fine-tuning a digital algorithm, streamlining a software tool, or elevating a user's experience, the feedback loop offers a systematic approach to consistently better results. In this discourse, we navigate the intricacies and transformative impact of this system.

Grasping the Concept of the Feedback Loop

Essentially, a feedback loop represents a recurring sequence in which the consequences or outcomes of a system are monitored and fed back into the system to influence subsequent results. Such loops can promote growth (positive feedback) or foster equilibrium and control (negative feedback).

Feedback Loop in Action

To illustrate, imagine a new digital tool released to a group of beta users. The feedback from these users, combined with recorded system metrics, forms the backbone of iterative improvement. Based on these insights, developers tweak the tool and launch an updated version. This cycle perpetuates, ushering in continuous enhancements.

Key Phases of the Feedback Loop

Gathering Data: It all begins with acquiring pertinent data, which could range from user experiences, system diagnostics, efficiency markers, to other relevant feedback that sheds light on the current system's efficacy.

Data Scrutiny: Post-collection, this data is meticulously assessed to identify patterns, inconsistencies, or potential improvements. With advanced tools like analytical software and AI-driven algorithms, even extensive datasets can yield meaningful information.

Modification Phase: Guided by the insights from the above analysis, changes are instituted in the system. This could be algorithmic alterations, user interface revamps, or any modifications aimed at optimization.

Review: After changes are executed, the system's new performance is gauged, laying the groundwork for the ensuing feedback cycle.

Why Iterative Refinement Matters

Ongoing Advancements: The foundational premise of feedback loops is perpetual enhancement. With each cycle, there's an opportunity to optimize further, bolstering efficiency, dependability, and user satisfaction.

Reduced Pitfalls: By recognizing and addressing potential snags early, the iterative process minimizes the risk of more pronounced setbacks or malfunctions.

Focus on the User: In systems that cater to end-users, feedback loops ensure that users' perspectives are integral, cultivating a more tailored and engaging experience.

Flexibility: Systems are equipped to be resilient and malleable in fluctuating environments, adjusting based on the latest feedback.

Potential Roadblocks

While replete with advantages, the feedback loop isn't without challenges:

Over-optimization: Especially with algorithms, there's a danger of becoming overly specialized to specific data, hindering its broader applicability.

Distinguishing Quality Feedback: All feedback isn't created equal. Sifting through the data to discern valuable insights from inconsequential feedback is paramount.

Temporal Gaps: Sometimes, the period between modifications and observing tangible results can be extended, slowing down the refinement and making causal relationships more opaque.

Balancing Diverse Feedback: In scenarios with varied stakeholder input, melding differing perspectives and prioritizing among contrasting recommendations becomes intricate.

Final Thoughts

The doctrine of feedback loops and iterative refinement, though rooted in engineering and control mechanisms, has permeated diverse spheres, from digital solutions to organizational frameworks. By assimilating its tenets and capitalizing on its strengths, entities across sectors can channel feedback's potential, propelling consistent advancements in their respective arenas.

Importance of A/B testing

In today's swiftly changing digital environment, businesses need to be agile and informed in their strategies. One method to stay ahead is A/B testing, a comparative assessment that juxtaposes two versions of a digital element to discern which performs optimally. This technique's value extends across several domains of digital strategy. Let's break down its core benefits.

A/B testing, sometimes termed split testing, is a method that compares two versions of a digital platform, such as a webpage or application, to see which one garners a better user response. The central charm of A/B testing lies in its directness. By tweaking a single component (like a content piece, layout, or button) and observing its influence on user engagement, businesses can progressively fine-tune their online assets.

Enhancing User Interaction

In a period where optimal user interaction is a benchmark of success, recognizing users' likes and dislikes is pivotal. A/B testing provides such knowledge. Through evaluating interactions with diverse versions of a platform, enterprises can discern what clicks with their users. Over time, these learnings can refine user experience, resulting in higher user retention and proactive interactions.

Decisions Anchored in Data

Reliance on intuition in digital strategies can lead to pitfalls. A/B testing sidesteps guesswork, replacing it with quantifiable data. When changes are underscored by tangible metrics, the guesswork gets eliminated, leading to decisions that resonate with genuine user preferences.

Risk Minimization

Unveiling a fresh design or feature without preliminary insights can be a dicey venture. A/B testing acts as a litmus test, letting businesses gauge user responses in a controlled setting before broad-scale implementation, mitigating potential adverse reactions.

Optimal Use of Resources

With numerous potential areas demanding investment in the digital domain, pinpointing the most impactful ones is essential. A/B testing offers clarity on which changes hold the most promise, ensuring resources are utilized where they matter most.

Discovering Unexpected Patterns

At times, subtle alterations can yield significant outcomes. A/B testing can spotlight these nuances. A slight change in a button's design or the semantics of a tagline might drastically boost user interactions. With consistent testing, these revelations can be effectively utilized.

Maintaining a Competitive Stance

To remain at the forefront in a dense digital marketplace, businesses need an edge. Regularly revisiting strategies through A/B testing ensures they are attuned to evolving user needs, helping businesses maintain their lead.

Concluding Thoughts

The digital arena, characterized by its fluidity, necessitates a structured, data-driven approach. A/B testing, through its focus on micro-level optimizations based on genuine user feedback, offers a roadmap. It empowers businesses to align their strategies with the pulse of their audience, ensuring continued relevance and resonance.

In an era marked by a deluge of digital platforms, aligning with user preferences isn't just beneficial; it's a mandate. A/B testing, with its detailed evaluation mechanism, is the key to unlocking this alignment, steering businesses towards informed, impactful decisions.

Metrics to evaluate prompt effectiveness

Within the world of conversational AI platforms, the potency of a dialogue heavily relies on the strength of the prompts guiding it. Prompt engineering is the art of steering AI toward desired, coherent responses. As we make strides in AI-driven dialogue technologies, understanding the efficiency of these prompts becomes crucial. Here, we delve into the pivotal metrics to assess the potency of prompts.

1. User Contentment Index (UCI)

Derived from post-engagement surveys or user feedback mechanisms, the UCI offers insights into user contentment post-interaction. A high index implies that the prompt appropriately directed the AI to deliver meaningful outcomes.

2. Pertinence Score

The essence of an AI conversation hinges on its relevance. The Pertinence Score gauges how well the AI's answer aligns with user inquiries. Evaluating this metric consistently allows for the identification and amelioration of misaligned prompts.

3. Interaction Success Rate

This metric monitors the frequency of successfully concluded user interactions without interruptions or premature endings. A sustained interaction hints at effective prompt guidance. A dwindling success rate could indicate suboptimal prompting or other conversational hiccups.

4. Rephrase Count

This metric focuses on the number of times a user must reword or repeat their query due to inadequate AI comprehension. Effective prompts should minimize this count, ensuring immediate comprehension.

5. Efficiency Measure

While this doesn't strictly gauge the AI's response quality, it measures the system's promptness. In interactive AI platforms, promptness is of the essence. Optimal prompts assist the AI in promptly sourcing the requisite data, ensuring swift outputs.

6. Interaction Mood Metrics

By leveraging natural language processing tools, one can deduce the mood of user feedback. High frequencies of positive moods can suggest successful prompting, while negative moods may hint at deficiencies in the prompting mechanism.

7. Secondary Inquiry Frequency

If users frequently need additional clarifications post an AI's reply, it might indicate that the primary response lacked thoroughness or precision. Prompt design can heavily influence this metric.

8. Target Fulfillment Index

For AI dialogues with distinct purposes, be it product guidance or troubleshooting, this index measures the success rate in achieving said purposes. Robust prompts will naturally steer users toward these ends, reflected in a high index value.

9. Human Transfer Quotient

In contexts like customer service bots, this quotient assesses how often users seek to transition from the bot to a human representative. An elevated quotient could suggest that the prompts aren't effectively catering to user requirements.

10. Response Variability Analysis

Analyzing the variety in AI outputs can offer insights into the effectiveness of the prompts. A monotonous, repetitive output for varying prompts can be indicative of the prompts not utilizing the AI's extensive database effectively.

11. Misstep Frequency

Inaccuracies, be they factual or contextual, can surface in AI outputs. Noting the occurrence of these can provide insights into potential areas of improvement in prompt design.

In Summation

The surge in conversational AI emphasizes the need for effective communication, with prompt engineering being its bedrock. Its success, though, hinges on continuous, metric-based assessments. The parameters highlighted here present a robust blueprint for such evaluations, ensuring AI dialogues are not just technologically apt but also resonate with user expectations. Assessing prompt potency is an evolving journey, critical to the dynamic enhancement of interactive AI systems.

Chapter Six

Advanced Prompt Techniques

Multi-modal prompts: Beyond just text

The evolution of conversational AI platforms has revolutionized the digital communication arena, predominantly through text-centric dialogues. However, as technology advances, there's a growing emphasis on diversifying modes of interaction. Multi-modal prompts have emerged as a key innovation, combining different sensory channels—visual, auditory, or even tactile—to enrich and diversify AI interactions.

1. Grasping the Multi-modal Concept

At its core, a multi-modal interface integrates data from multiple modes or channels. Rather than being limited to text, it capitalizes on images, sounds, touch signals, and more to decipher and formulate responses. This convergence results in a more comprehensive and organic interaction environment, closely resembling human interactions.

2. Tapping into the Visual Domain

Images and graphics are primary sources of contextual information. Modern multi-modal systems can be initiated using pictures, clips, or visual diagrams. Consider a hypothetical scenario with an AI-powered medical helper. A user might share an image of a symptom, and when combined with text descriptors, the AI offers a more refined opinion.

3. Auditory Channels in Play

Incorporating sound-based cues deepens the AI's ability to discern nuances. The subtleties of voice, background sounds, and vocal fluctuations can be invaluable. In scenarios like customer feedback, understanding a user's mood through their tone can help the AI respond more effectively.

4. The Role of Touch and Physical Feedback

Thanks to breakthroughs in haptic innovations, touch offers a fresh dimension for AI interactions. In realms like immersive gaming or specialist training tools, touch feedback enhances user engagement. Using this tactile data, AI systems can adjust and fine-tune future interactions.

5. Advantages of Multi-modal Interactions

Augmented Precision: Drawing from diverse data sources enables AI systems to comprehend context more deeply, yielding accurate outcomes.

Minimizing Uncertainty: A potential vagueness in one mode can be offset by clarity from another, such as a muffled voice command being supplemented with text.

Engaging Interaction: Multi-modal prompts give users a plethora of options for conveying their messages, resulting in dynamic engagements.

Ensuring Accessibility: Given the varied preferences of users, some might opt for voice due to specific constraints, while others might choose images. Multi-modal platforms ensure accessibility for all.

6. Navigating Multi-modal Implementation Challenges

Handling Abundant Data: Processing and interpreting vast and varied data from several channels can be daunting.

Achieving Cohesion: Maintaining fluidity and coordination between diverse channels is crucial. Any misalignment can jeopardize the interaction's quality.

System Intricacy: Designing algorithms to manage several data streams introduces heightened complexity.

Security and Privacy: The broader the data range, the more imperative the need for robust security protocols.

7. Forward Momentum

With breakthroughs in technologies like augmented and virtual reality, the scope for immersive multi-modal interactions has expanded considerably. Furthermore, as newer technologies like 5G become mainstream, the processing of diverse data in real-time will become more efficient, setting the stage for instantaneous, immersive AI communications.

Concluding Thoughts

The shift in digital communications is not just about data exchange but about enriching user experiences. Multi-modal prompts are leading this transformative journey, offering interactions that are not just effective but also deeply human-like. By extending beyond the textual realm, they promise a future of interactions that are intuitive, inclusive, and deeply contextual, redefining the future of AI-driven communications.

Conditional and dynamic prompts

In the ever-expanding world of conversational AI, producing user interactions that are both nuanced and contextually accurate is of paramount importance. Key to achieving this are conditional and dynamic prompts, which equip AI models to deliver adaptable, context-rich responses. In this discussion, we will explore the deeper layers of these prompts, emphasizing their value and functionality in enriching the quality of AI-user dialogues.

Decoding Conditional Prompts

At their core, conditional prompts operate based on the logic of "if this, then that." Essentially, they determine the course of the conversation based on certain set criteria or user inputs. Think of them as navigational beacons in the domain of AI discourse, directing the interaction as per specific guidelines or conditions.

To illustrate, within a retail chatbot framework, a query about the warranty of a gadget would lead the system, conditioned with a certain prompt, to furnish details aligned with gadget warranties. If the query then zooms into a specific brand, the conditional prompt can fine-tune its response to cater to that particular brand's warranty clauses.

The Evolution to Dynamic Prompts

Where conditional prompts steer the dialogue based on pre-set criteria, dynamic prompts take a more agile approach. They conjure up responses in real-time, factoring in various elements like user behavior, prior interactions, current context, or even live data streams.

Let's consider a hotel booking chatbot. A dynamic prompt within this system might mesh together live room availability, the user's historical preferences, and any ongoing deals to craft a bespoke response, ensuring it's not just factual but also individualized.

Behind-the-Curtains Mechanics

Tapping External Sources: Dynamic prompts often draw from external data reservoirs or web-based services. They can pull in instantaneous data – say, traffic updates or event schedules – to make the interaction more informative.

Capitalizing on History: Advanced AI architectures, particularly those rooted in neural networks, utilize recent interactions to forge more in-context responses. For instance, if a user has shown interest in gluten-free eateries, a subsequent query about local specialties might emphasize gluten-free options.

Anticipatory Analytics: Some prompts are predictive in nature, gauging possible user queries or needs based on the ongoing conversation and other relevant data points.

Merits of Conditional and Dynamic Prompts

Context-Centricity: By adjusting to explicit conditions or molding responses around a blend of variables, these prompts assure AI dialogues that align closely with user intent and context.

Elevated User Engagement: Interactions that are both intuitive and tailored significantly enhance user contentment. An AI's knack to "recall" or "tune into" the progression of the dialogue ensures smoother exchanges, reducing redundancies.

Efficiency Boost: On the enterprise front, these advanced prompts can offload a considerable burden from customer service representatives. With their capability to address intricate queries and even foresee user requirements, they can autonomously manage a vast majority of user touchpoints.

Challenges on the Horizon

However, the pathway to implementing these prompts isn't devoid of hurdles.

Design Intricacies: Architecting effective conditional prompts demands a thorough comprehension of potential user journeys. It's an intensive endeavor that necessitates rigorous strategizing and frequent refinement.

Straddling Personalization: Personalization stands as the hallmark of dynamic prompts, but there's a balance to strike. It's essential to respect user privacy and ensure responses don't come across as overly probing.

Deciphering Vagueness: Owing to their adaptive nature, dynamic prompts must contend with vague user inputs. The art lies in equipping them to seek further clarification when confronted with ambiguities.

To Conclude

In the intricate world of conversational AI, conditional and dynamic prompts emerge as potent tools, orchestrating dialogues that reflect depth and adaptability. By harmonizing pre-defined logic with real-time agility, they pave the way for interactions that resonate with human-like discernment and fluidity. As we march forward into the future of AI, honing these prompts will be instrumental in shaping AI conversations that are even more user-aligned and intuitive.

Leveraging external data for prompts

In the rapidly evolving landscape of conversational AI, the aptitude to employ external data sources to shape and guide dialogues stands as a game-changer. Such an approach not only amplifies the precision and relevance of the interactions but also elevates the end-user experience. This exploration focuses on the criticality, methodologies, and challenges surrounding the use of external datasets to improve the richness of prompts within AI-driven chat interfaces.

The Rationale Behind External Data Utilization

Conversational AI models are traditionally molded by vast training datasets. These foundational datasets, albeit expansive, might lack up-to-the-minute or niche-specific insights. External data bridges this gap:

Timely Insights: Industries like meteorology, finance, or media are characterized by fleeting updates. By incorporating real-time data channels, AI tools can provide instant, relevant feedback.

Depth of Context: Tapping into continuously updated reservoirs, such as scientific repositories or evolving market insights, allows AI to deliver current and in-depth responses.

Tailored User Engagement: Accessing user-centric data, like transaction records or user preferences (with appropriate permissions), ensures personalized and resonant AI-user dialogues.

Mechanisms for External Data Assimilation

Various strategies can be adopted to integrate external data, each with its distinct characteristics:

Interfacing through APIs: A widespread approach involves AI systems interfacing with dedicated APIs (Application Programming Interfaces) to pull contemporary or specific data. For example, a chatbot catering to travel queries might draw from flight status APIs for real-time updates.

Web Data Extraction: Although not always the optimal or ethical choice, certain systems might resort to web scraping to glean data from online content in the absence of an API.

Direct Database Linkages: In scenarios where institutions manage comprehensive data reservoirs, providing the AI direct access can streamline data retrieval.

Factors for Deliberation

Integrating external datasets does come with its set of challenges and considerations:

Integrity and Quality of Data: It's pivotal to vet external sources for reliability and accuracy to circumvent the risk of misinformation.

Potential Latency Issues: Fetching data in real-time might introduce delays, especially if there are server constraints or network issues.

Ethical and Privacy Aspects: When handling sensitive or personal data, adherence to privacy standards and ethical norms becomes non-negotiable.

Economic Considerations: Accessing some data streams or APIs might incur costs, necessitating a cost-benefit analysis.

Availability and Backup: To guarantee uninterrupted service, having alternate data sources or resorting to cached data for scenarios where primary sources falter is advisable.

The Evolving Dynamics

The confluence of AI-generated prompts with external data repositories has ushered in a new era:

Dialogues with Depth: By deriving insights from external sources, AI-driven interactions transcend traditional knowledge limits, ensuring users are equipped with fresh and context-relevant details.

Building User Confidence: Sourcing from reputable external pools can enhance user trust in AI-sourced responses.

Diverse Application Realms: The fusion allows for diverse applications, from offering real-time market analyses to real-time health advisories based on current research.

Wrapping Up

The rise of conversational AI accentuates the importance of a symbiotic relationship between embedded AI knowledge and the expansive world of external data. Utilizing external data for prompts is evolving from being an added feature to a crucial aspect. By integrating the two harmoniously, we move closer to the ideal: designing AI platforms that are not only well-informed but are also adaptive, responsive, and consistently updated.

Chapter Seven

Overcoming Challenges in Prompt Engineering

Handling unexpected user responses

Conversational AI, despite its advancements, grapples with the inherent unpredictability of human interactions. Every user, with their unique background and intent, can introduce queries or comments that a data model might not be prepared for. Addressing these unforeseen responses, while ensuring seamless user experience, necessitates a nuanced approach. In this analysis, we'll explore the importance of managing unexpected user inputs and the methodologies to bolster the robustness of AI-driven conversation tools.

Deciphering the Nature of Unexpected Inputs

It's essential first to understand what constitutes 'unexpected' interactions. These can include:

Varied Expressions: Users might communicate familiar ideas using distinct vernaculars or jargon.

Vague Statements: Questions or comments that are either too broad or can be taken in multiple directions.

Input Errors: Typos, syntax errors, or phrases that don't align semantically.

Beyond-the-Scope Questions: Inquiries that stray from the chatbot's designated expertise or domain.

Sentiment-Heavy Inputs: Expressions of strong emotion, sarcasm, or humor that might not be immediately discernible to the system.

Strategies for Addressing Unanticipated Interactions

Effective Fallback Protocols: Having a default strategy is imperative. If uncertain, the system can admit its limitations. Sentences like "I'm unsure about that. Let's try another topic," can pivot the conversation back to familiar grounds without causing user dissatisfaction.

Continuous Enhancement: Treat every unanticipated input as a chance to grow. By consistently monitoring and assessing these inputs, developers can fine-tune the model for better accuracy over time.

Retention of Dialogue Context: Ensure the system has a memory of past exchanges. This historical context can be instrumental in providing apt responses, even when the immediate user input seems incongruous.

Hierarchical Response Approach: Adopt a tiered strategy. Aim first to discern the user's intent. If this proves challenging, the system should then move to its fallback response. This approach ensures optimal effort before resorting to a more general reply.

Soliciting User Insights: Enable users to offer feedback on their conversational experiences. This direct feedback loop can be critical in enhancing system resilience.

Recognizing and Adapting to User Emotions: Equip the system with emotion detection mechanisms. By identifying sentiments like frustration, the AI can adjust its tone or even suggest escalating the query to a human counterpart.

Marrying Automated Systems with Human Oversight

In high-stakes situations, such as medical or financial consultations, a hybrid model combining AI responsiveness with human monitoring can be beneficial. Transitioning challenging interactions to human representatives ensures accuracy and builds user trust.

The Ethics of Interaction

Addressing unexpected interactions is not just about system capabilities; it touches on ethical considerations as well. It's essential for systems to recognize and respect user sensitivities, especially when discussions venture into personal territories. For topics of a sensitive nature, the AI should tread lightly, offering general responses while advocating for expert intervention if needed.

Concluding Thoughts

Building a resilient dialogue system equipped to tackle unforeseen user interactions is a continuous endeavor. It calls for technological acumen, human intuition, and a profound grasp of user nuances. As the role of AI expands across various sectors, refining its capacity to interact authentically and meaningfully with users will be of paramount importance. Embracing the challenge of the unexpected is the pathway to creating truly transformative conversational experiences.

Managing cultural and linguistic nuances

Effective conversational AI's global deployment is contingent not only on technological sophistication but also on its aptitude to align with users from varied linguistic and cultural spectra. Given the intricate nuances, cultural connotations, and idiomatic expressions intrinsic to languages, the crafting of universally efficient AI systems mandates an in-depth comprehension and adept management of these facets.

Unraveling Linguistic Complexities

Languages, shaped by myriad historical, societal, and cultural determinants, go beyond mere semantic components; they encapsulate shared values, beliefs, and societal perspectives.

Idiomatic Challenges: Idiomatic phrases often defy direct translation. An English phrase like "kick the bucket" might be misunderstood if translated verbatim into another language.

Varied Meanings: Semantic values of words can shift based on context. "Bank," for example, can indicate a financial institution or the side of a river, depending on its application.

Differing Sentiment Connotations: A word that's perceived positively in one cultural context might be neutral or even negative in another.

Navigating Cultural Undercurrents

Beyond linguistic intricacies, cultural underpinnings significantly influence communicative dynamics. Conversational systems must be acutely aware of societal mores, rituals, and potential red zones.

Expressions of Respect: Different cultures have varied ways to convey respect. Some use specific verb forms, while others may employ particular titles or phrases.

Navigating Societal Sensitivities: It's crucial for systems to be attuned to topics that may be touchy or contentious in certain regions.

Acknowledgment of Local Traditions: Incorporating knowledge of local holidays and customs can make AI interactions more engaging and relatable.

Effective Approaches to Handle Linguistic and Cultural Diversities

Region-Specific Systems: Rather than a universal model, there's merit in developing systems attuned to specific linguistic or regional demographics.

Adaptive Learning Models: The evolving nature of language and societal norms necessitates that conversational interfaces be adaptive and up-to-date.

Human Oversight: While automation is efficient, human intervention is sometimes essential to mediate and ensure the subtleties are adequately addressed.

Expanding Interaction Channels: Augmenting text with voice and possibly visual interactions can help discern and relay nuances better.

User-Centric Feedback: Enabling users to flag or correct responses enhances the system's accuracy and sensitivity over time.

Moral Imperatives

Navigating linguistic and cultural terrains isn't solely a technical endeavor; it has moral ramifications. Any oversight can reinforce clichés or unintentionally alienate users. It's paramount to ensure that conversational systems foster inclusivity and respect.

In Summation

In an interconnected world where AI has the potential to be a unifying force, addressing linguistic and cultural subtleties is crucial. This journey demands an amalgamation of technological prowess, linguistic insights, cultural anthropology, and ethical considerations. Embracing the multifaceted dimensions of human communication will ensure AI systems that are more effective, empathetic, and inclusive.

Addressing biases in prompts

The emergence and proliferation of artificial intelligence systems in modern sectors means these tools mirror the data they've learned from. Given the omnipresence of AI across various domains ranging from medicine to media, it's essential to ensure these systems offer unbiased responses. This is crucial when considering prompts, which are central to user interaction. Ensuring that biases in prompts are addressed is more than a technical issue; it's a societal responsibility to guarantee that AI tools serve every user equitably.

1. Deciphering the Essence of Biases

In the AI landscape, bias refers to unwarranted or persistent differences in system outputs. Such discrepancies can arise from multiple areas:

Skewed Training Data: If biases infest the initial data feeding the AI, then the resulting model will likely mirror these inclinations.

Lack of Diverse Representation: Absence of diverse inputs can cause the system to misinterpret or overlook certain user groups.

Cyclic Biases: Biases can amplify when AI systems undergo refinements based on user feedback without proper scrutiny.

2. Consequences of Bias-laden Prompts

Biased AI prompts have repercussions that extend beyond mere inaccuracies:

Perpetuating Stereotypes: Such prompts can inadvertently strengthen societal preconceptions, fueling further miscommunication.

Economic Outcomes: In areas like employment or finance, these biases can translate into tangible negative outcomes.

Eroding User Confidence: For AI to become integral, user trust is essential. Biases can jeopardize this trust, hindering widespread acceptance of AI solutions.

3. Holistic Approaches to Bias Reduction

Addressing biases requires a comprehensive strategy:

Broad Data Gathering: Ensuring the data is sourced from varied and diverse origins can help alleviate inherent biases.

Periodic Assessments: Regularly evaluating AI outputs for biases, possibly with independent audits, is imperative.

Employing Fairness Protocols: Emerging research focuses on ensuring AI fairness. Adopting these protocols can be proactive in bias reduction.

Refining Prompt Construction: Re-evaluating and ensuring prompts are unbiased can significantly reduce the chance of slanted results.

4. The Critical Role of Human Intervention

Despite AI's automated nature, human judgment remains a cornerstone, especially in detecting and rectifying biases:

Validation with Human Experts: Engaging experts trained in bias identification can aid in neutralizing the initial data.

Human-monitored Systems: Systems allowing real-time human corrections can effectively reduce bias in outputs.

5. The Case for Transparency and User Engagement

Open dialogue about the potential for biases and measures to counteract them is essential:

Open Methodologies: Disclosing AI training processes and data sources can provide users with an understanding of potential biases.

Encouraging User Feedback: Systems where users can highlight biases can enhance trust and assist in refining AI responses.

6. Ethical Considerations and Regulatory Aspects

Bias correction extends beyond technical accuracy to ethical obligation:

Adhering to Ethical Standards: Organizations should define and follow ethical principles concerning AI fairness.

Governmental Standards: Regulatory entities can provide a framework for ensuring AI tools uphold fairness standards.

Conclusion

Ensuring bias-free prompts in AI is a continuous process that intertwines technology, human discernment, ethical standards, and feedback loops. As AI's footprint expands across sectors, achieving unbiased, transparent, and fair interactions isn't just an aspiration but a mandate. This commitment will cement AI's role as a positive, enhancing force in human interactions, ensuring equity for all its users.

Chapter Eight

Tools and Technologies for Prompt Engineering

Overview of available tools for crafting and testing prompts

The fusion of linguistic artistry with computational prowess has given birth to the domain of prompt engineering. Its objective? To enrich human-artificial intelligence interaction by eliciting more nuanced outputs from machine learning frameworks. With the rising demand for specialized prompt crafting and testing, a myriad of tools has emerged. This article delves into some of these pivotal tools, shedding light on their capabilities and functionalities.

1. Crafting Prompts: Instruments at Hand:

ChatGPT Playground: A user-friendly interface that encourages users to tinker with diverse prompts, providing instant feedback on how models react. An invaluable resource for novices, it underscores the importance of word choice in shaping AI reactions.

ParlAI: An innovation by Facebook AI Research, ParlAI serves as a hub for training and evaluating dialogue-centric models. Its in-built tools and expansive dataset collection make it a favorite for those keen on mastering the nuances of prompt crafting.

Rasa NLU: With an emphasis on comprehending natural language, Rasa NLU is a tool that aids in training models to pinpoint user intent and categorize entities, essential for intent-driven prompts.

2. Testing Tools for Polishing Prompts:

Botpress: A holistic platform, Botpress not only supports conversational AI development but also offers real-time testing environments, ensuring that prompts stand up to real-world scrutiny.

Dialogflow CX: A product of Google's innovation, this tool allows intricate conversational pathways to be visualized and tested. It enables prompt engineers to appreciate the ripple effect of their crafted stimuli on dialogue trajectories.

Microsoft Bot Framework: Beyond facilitating chatbot development, this suite provides a local testing environment. It ensures that prompts are refined to perfection before they're broadcasted to the world.

3. Analytical Tools: Assessing Prompt Impact:

TensorBoard: Complementing TensorFlow, this visualization tool offers an inside look into how model performance correlates with prompt structure, offering valuable insights to refine the crafting process.

Wit.ai: Beyond its primary function of translating speech or text to structured data, Wit.ai's analytical prowess can shed light on a prompt's efficacy in data extraction.

4. Multimodal Prompt Crafting:

DeepAI Text to Image API: A unique tool that translates textual descriptions into visual counterparts, providing an avenue for those keen on exploring prompts that tap into both visual and textual modalities.

Affectiva: Pioneering in the realm of emotion AI, Affectiva offers a window into how facial expressions react to prompts, paving the way for emotion-centric prompt design.

5. Collective Platforms for Collaborative Crafting:

GitHub: While its primary function is code collaboration, GitHub hosts a wealth of repositories dedicated to the art and science of prompt engineering, encouraging community-driven refinement.

PaperSpace: Tailored for machine learning endeavors, this platform offers shared spaces, allowing prompt enthusiasts to collaborate, experiment, and iterate together.

Conclusion:

Prompt engineering, as a field, is rapidly evolving, buoyed by a suite of sophisticated tools. From crafting and testing to analyzing and refining, every step of the journey is supported. As AI models continue to reshape the digital interaction landscape, expertly designed prompts will play an even more crucial role. With the tools highlighted above, prompt engineers are well-equipped to lead this transformation, ensuring that interactions remain not only precise but also engaging and context-aware

Integration with existing AI dialogue systems

In today's fast-paced technological landscape, dialogue systems play a pivotal role in shaping the interface between humans and computers. While these systems are powerful on their own, weaving them seamlessly into existing AI structures amplifies their capabilities manifold. This piece aims to elucidate the nuances of such integrations, addressing the inherent hurdles, methodologies, and the value they bring to the table.

Peering into the World of AI Dialogue Systems:

At their essence, AI dialogue systems are crafted to facilitate organic and fluid conversations with humans. Supported by sophisticated algorithms, they can process user inputs, retrieve necessary data, and formulate pertinent responses. Their utility spans across diverse domains, from customer service chatbots to intelligent virtual aides in digital devices.

Why Integration is Crucial:

The contemporary technological and business milieu is peppered with a variety of AI-driven tools, each catering to specific functions like data processing, visual recognition, or gauging sentiments. For a holistic user experience, it is vital that dialogue systems cohesively blend with these elements.

Consistent Interaction Experience: By integrating dialogue systems with other AI tools, users can enjoy a harmonized and consistent interaction, irrespective of the nature of their query or transaction.

Immediate Data Retrieval: A well-integrated system can instantaneously fetch data from various tools, whether they are customer relationship management systems, inventory databases, or analytical insights, providing users with timely and relevant data.

Heightened Personalization: Accessing data from integrated sources enables dialogue systems to tailor conversations based on a user's historical data, real-time sentiments, or behavioral patterns, establishing a unique user-centric approach.

Pathways to Fluid Integration:

Leveraging APIs and Webhooks: Contemporary AI solutions often come equipped with APIs that facilitate integration. Similarly, webhooks can be utilized to initiate real-time communication between platforms, enabling dialogue systems to engage with other platforms effectively.

Utilizing Bridging Platforms: Solutions like Zapier or Microsoft Power Automate can act as conduits, ensuring data flows smoothly between dialogue systems and other platforms, even for those without extensive technical know-how.

Bespoke Integration: For intricate or legacy system integrations, specialized coding might be the way forward. This would involve developing tailored scripts to foster communication between the dialogue system and other platforms.

Potential Roadblocks:

Despite the array of advantages, integration comes with its set of challenges:

Upholding Data Integrity: With dialogue systems interfacing with multiple platforms, maintaining robust security protocols is vital. Ensuring that each integration point is shielded from vulnerabilities is paramount.

Mitigating Delays: Seamless data sharing and communication might introduce delays. Optimizations are essential to guarantee prompt and efficient user interactions.

Ensuring Uniformity: When multiple platforms collaborate, it's crucial to establish and adhere to consistent standards and procedures, preventing any inconsistencies that might disrupt the user journey.

A Glimpse Ahead:

The ever-increasing capabilities of AI demand that integration becomes a standard practice. As AI dialogue systems advance, their interplay with other systems will only grow more intricate and adaptive. We're progressing towards a unified AI ecosystem where distinct components seamlessly merge, functioning in perfect harmony.

Wrapping Up:

Embedding AI dialogue systems within the broader AI framework, though challenging, paves the way for an enhanced user experience characterized by real-time feedback, tailored interactions, and consistent support. As the AI realm expands, perfecting integration techniques will be instrumental in tapping into its immense promise.

Importance of continuous integration and deployment

In today's rapidly evolving software development landscape, agility, reliability, and timeliness are crucial. To meet these demands, outdated software release methods are being overshadowed by more progressive practices: Continuous Integration (CI) and Continuous Deployment (CD). These methods are reshaping how developers design, test, and roll out software.

Continuous Integration: A Collaborative Approach

Continuous Integration involves consistently integrating code modifications into a central repository. This frequent merging, mostly automated, ensures smooth amalgamation of code contributions from various developers.

Real-Time Feedback Mechanism: A hallmark of CI is its capability to provide instantaneous feedback to developers. As developers commit code, automated testing immediately signals any discrepancies. This real-time detection streamlines the debugging process, conserving both time and effort.

Consistent Code Caliber: Regular code integrations diminish the intricacies of combining diverse code chunks. This rhythm not only reduces integration challenges but also maintains a high standard of code quality. Moreover, automated testing confirms that newly added modifications don't infringe on pre-existing functions.

Team Synergy and Visibility: CI fosters a team environment where developers routinely share their work. This synchronization enhances team transparency and cultivates a sense of shared ownership of the project.

Continuous Deployment: Elevating Integration

Continuous Deployment builds upon CI principles. In this approach, every modification that clears the automated tests is automatically moved to the production environment, eradicating the need for manual intervention.

Accelerated Release Turnaround: The standout benefit of CD is the velocity at which updates, fixes, or new features reach the end-users. This ensures users continuously access the freshest version of the software.

Minimized Deployment Hazards: Traditional deployment techniques, with extended gaps between rollouts, introduce numerous changes at once. In contrast, CD's regular releases ensure modifications are gradual and manageable, reducing deployment-associated risks.

User-Driven Development: The regularity of CD allows for a swift response to user feedback, ensuring the software consistently mirrors user desires and expectations.

CI/CD: A Harmonious Fusion

While CI and CD can stand alone, their combined force, represented as CI/CD, delivers a cohesive procedure from code creation to its deployment.

Optimized Operations: CI/CD removes the monotony of repetitive tasks, mitigating human errors, and trimming the duration from code conception to its deployment. This streamlining enables developers to channel their efforts towards creative solutions.

Economical Operations: Detecting errors early with CI/CD reduces the financial strains linked with protracted debugging and extensive post-launch patches.

Adaptability and Robustness: Modern CI/CD platforms cater to both compact and expansive teams, ensuring adaptability. Moreover, they guarantee a resilient infrastructure equipped with contingency measures like rollback options for unforeseen complications.

Wrapping Up

Continuous Integration and Continuous Deployment signify more than just innovative operational methods; they embody a transformative philosophy in software creation and dissemination. Integrating CI/CD assures that organizations stay nimble, user-aligned, and ahead in a domain marked by shifting user preferences and technological breakthroughs. As digital solutions permeate every business aspect, the tenets of CI and CD will become indispensable for organizations aspiring for consistent advancement and ingenuity.

Chapter Nine

Ethical Considerations in Prompt Design

Addressing biases: Gender, race, and more

As we navigate the digital epoch, algorithms have emerged as the underpinning of many of our technological breakthroughs. Ranging from the realms of search utilities and digital social spheres to innovative healthcare and public safety solutions, the footprint of machine learning and artificial intelligence is undeniable. Yet, with this expansion comes a series of challenges. At the forefront of these challenges is the pressing concern of biases, particularly when gender, race, and other societal markers come into play.

Origins of Biased Algorithms

Data Sources: The essence of machine learning algorithms, inclusive of deep learning structures, hinges on the neutrality of their training data. When this data captures societal disparities, like those rooted in gender or race, it is reflected in the algorithmic outputs, often reinforcing and sometimes magnifying them.

Assumptions in Design: In attempts to model the intricacies of the real world, algorithms may inadvertently lean towards a specific demographic, resulting in imbalances.

Bias in Practice

Gender-Related Biases: Recruitment AIs have, on occasion, demonstrated a bias towards male applicants for tech-based roles over female counterparts of equal merit. Similarly, voice-driven systems, primarily trained on male voice data, have occasionally faltered with female intonations.

Ethnicity-Based Biases: There have been reported cases where certain face recognition tools have inaccurately identified individuals from specific ethnic backgrounds more than others. Moreover, some data-driven law enforcement tools have disproportionately targeted areas based on possibly prejudiced historical data.

Economic and Additional Biases: Biases aren't restricted to race and gender. For instance, algorithms dictating credit scores might inadvertently marginalize specific income brackets, and some healthcare tools might unintentionally de-prioritize certain patient groups.

Strategies for Bias Reduction

Transparent Data Origins: It's vital for AI developers to understand the source of their datasets and any inherent predispositions. Initiating with data that is annotated with relevant metadata concerning its origin and potential biases sets the stage.

Inclusive Training Data: Making sure that datasets cover a broad spectrum of potential user categories can alleviate ingrained biases. For example, a facial detection tool, when trained on faces from varied ethnicities and age groups, is less prone to errors.

Routine System Checks: Periodic reviews and assessments of AI solutions can identify and rectify unintended biases. Such evaluations, preferably by independent entities, can ensure the system's input and output fairness.

Algorithms for Bias Identification: Emerging technologies are now tailoring algorithms to identify potential biases in other machine processes. These algorithms evaluate outputs across various user groups to guarantee equal representation.

Engaging Varied Stakeholders: Drawing insights from a mix of AI engineers, users, ethical scholars, and those directly impacted by the AI decisions can foster a comprehensive understanding of the AI's real-world repercussions.

Moral Responsibility

Beyond the realm of technicalities, addressing biases in AI resonates as a moral obligation. Every decision swayed by bias, from misidentifying an individual to withholding an opportunity, resonates in the real world. Thus, the quest for impartial AI transcends mere technical refinement; it touches upon ensuring equitable opportunities in a world increasingly steered by automation.

In Summation

The reflection of societal biases in AI underlines the pervasive nature of these prejudices. However, with conscious effort, vigilance, and utilizing the right methodologies, the tech industry has the potential to counteract these biases. As we edge into an AI-dominated future, our proactive measures now will decide if this technology will perpetuate disparities or herald a more balanced and just society.

Ensuring user privacy and data security

In today's interconnected digital era, prioritizing user privacy and fortifying data security is of utmost significance. The proliferation of digital tools and AI-centric applications across various domains has accentuated the importance of robust data protection mechanisms. While modern technologies have brought numerous conveniences to our fingertips, they also usher in challenges related to potential data exploitation. Navigating these challenges calls for a thorough grasp of possible risks and the adoption of comprehensive measures to counter them.

Origins of Digital Exposure

Diverse Digital Interactions: People's engagement with an array of digital services, from online shopping platforms to telemedicine apps, has amplified. Each of these engagements, if inadequately shielded, can become a conduit for data compromise.

Evolution of Cyber Threats: The realm of cyber threats has witnessed rapid evolution. Intricate methods like Advanced Persistent Threats (APTs), malware, and spear-phishing are examples of techniques used by adversaries to penetrate data sanctuaries.

Facets of User Privacy

Selective Data Collection: Restricting data acquisition to only essential attributes is pivotal. Gathering excessive data not only undermines user confidence but also broadens the window of susceptibility.

Informed Choice and Autonomy: Users must be thoroughly apprised of data utilization intentions and should have authority over their data, including access, amendment, and deletion rights.

Data Masking and Ciphering: Making intercepted data uninterpretable is key. Methods such as data masking, which obscures personal data elements, and ciphering, which scrambles the data, deter unauthorized exploitation.

Blueprints for Secure Data Handling

Multifaceted Security Arrangements: This concept, often referred to as a multi-tiered defense, involves instituting a plethora of security measures. By doing so, the failure of one defense layer doesn't compromise the entire system.

Periodic Security Scrutiny and Vulnerability Assessments: Taking a proactive stance to identify system weak spots is essential. Routine cybersecurity reviews, paired with vulnerability assessments involving ethical hacking, shed light on potential system fragilities.

Ongoing System Surveillance: Constant system oversight can swiftly spot and rectify anomalies. Any unauthorized intrusion or aberrant data transfer can be immediately flagged.

Data Preservation and Restoration: Maintaining data wholesomeness is as essential as its safeguarding. Periodic data archiving, preferably in varied locations, ensures data accessibility. Effective data recovery systems come into play in the face of breaches or technical glitches.

Workforce Enlightenment: Human lapses often become system vulnerabilities. Educating the workforce about cybersecurity best practices, like discerning phishing endeavors and maintaining secure communications, reduces risk exposure.

Regulatory Adherence: Universal protocols like Europe's General Data Protection Regulation (GDPR) or the United States' California Consumer Privacy Act (CCPA) outline data protection norms. Conforming to these guidelines not only ensures legal propriety but also fosters user confidence.

Designing with the User in Mind

Adopting a user-oriented design philosophy emphasizes the crucial role users play in the digital ecosystem. Empowering users with tools and insights allows them to discern the ramifications of their online actions.

Clear Disclosure Practices: Users should be apprised, using simple and straightforward language, about how their data is processed, its objectives, and any third-party involvements.

Intuitive Security Measures: Implementing user-friendly security measures, such as biometric checks, dual-factor verification, and robust password guidelines, ensures easier user compliance and thus wider adoption.

Concluding Thoughts

Protecting user privacy and ensuring data security transcends mere technical hurdles. They emerge as moral imperatives for all digital service providers. As the digital realm continues to grow, a vigilant and holistic approach to these concerns will dictate the reliability and longevity of online platforms and utilities.

The line between helpful and intrusive AI

As we steer through this digital age, AI has undeniably carved its niche, proposing myriad solutions aimed at refining our daily undertakings. From digital aides and suggestion systems to adept anticipatory analytics, AI's influence is embedded in our contemporary routines. But, this technological marvel poses an intricate question: At what point does AI, meant to be an ally, verge on becoming too prying?

AI's Journey: A Dual-Faceted Narrative

AI's dawn was met with applause for its revolutionary potential. Actions that traditionally required significant human effort—like sifting through vast data or mundane chores like calendar management—were suddenly executed with unparalleled efficiency. These systems held the promise of self-evolution, adaptability, and decision-making grounded in extensive data pools.

However, this prowess is a double-edged sword. As AI frameworks become more intricate, their data demands surge.

The quest for unparalleled AI performance has inadvertently birthed an insatiable quest for intimate and detailed data.

Defining the Thin Line: Utility vs. Overreach

To truly grasp AI's reach, we need to discern between its beneficial aspects and its overstepping bounds.

Customized Solutions vs. Privacy Dilemmas: The allure of AI is its capacity for bespoke user experiences. From music selections to tailored shopping suggestions, AI crafts these based on a user's history. But this customization hinges on having deep access to user interactions and sometimes even personal conversations. The line blurs when users feel over-scrutinized, leading to discomfort and mistrust.

Anticipatory Insights vs. Overzealous Decisions: AI's predictive potential can map out likely future trends based on past data. This is invaluable in fields like healthcare. But problems arise when AI starts preemptively acting on behalf of users, stripping them of their autonomy.

Efficient Automation vs. Unwarranted Dominance: AI's capability to automate is revolutionary, simplifying complex processes across sectors. However, the issue surfaces when automation extends beyond its mandate, taking unsolicited decisions or negating human preferences.

Ethical Paradigms: Seeking Permission and Openness

Central to AI's deployment is an underlying ethical foundation.

Seeking Permission: Users should have a crystal-clear understanding of how AI will handle their data. Concealed clauses or ambiguities undercut the principle of genuine agreement. Users should be at the forefront of any data decision.

Openness: It's essential to shed light on the workings of AI—the decision-making process, data sources, and inherent predispositions. Concealing these elements erodes trust.

The Road Ahead: A Unified Strategy

Harnessing AI's prowess while honoring its limitations demands a joint effort:

Governance Entities: It's imperative to shape dynamic, comprehensive regulations that address AI's evolving landscape. Such guidelines should champion user safety without curtailing progress.

AI Designers and Corporations: Ethical considerations should be integral to AI's developmental phase. A user-first approach emphasizing consent and clarity should be paramount.

General Public: Knowledge empowers. The masses need to be informed about AI's potential and boundaries. By understanding and tweaking AI's functionalities, they can retain control over their data narratives.

In Summary

While AI holds the potential to sculpt a streamlined, progressive future, its deployment demands meticulous scrutiny. The challenge transcends mere technological boundaries, delving into moral terrain. By collaboratively delineating between AI's beneficial attributes and its overreaching tendencies, we can usher in an epoch where technology amplifies human potential without overshadowing personal freedoms.

Chapter Ten

Case Studies in Effective Prompt Engineering

Real-world examples of good and bad prompts

The digital realm is laden with myriad touchpoints where interactions blossom, often triggered by prompts. These brief messages aim to steer users towards designated tasks or deliver essential insights. Masterfully constructed, they become instrumental in fostering engagement. Yet, if mishandled, they can obscure the message and aggravate users. A deep dive into actual experiences can shed light on the art and science of prompt design.

Well-Executed Prompts: Markers of Proficiency

E-commerce Shopping Aid:

Prompt: "Seems you've not completed your purchase. Care to finalize your order?"

Interpretation: This prompt is a masterstroke of relevancy and timing. Drawing attention to potentially overlooked items, it tactfully nudges users towards transaction closure without appearing forceful.

Software Enhancement Alert:

Prompt: "An upgraded version is ready for you. Fancy updating now or prefer a later reminder?"

Interpretation: This prompt wisely offers users a choice—to proceed with the update or delay it, thereby acknowledging their current engagement while highlighting the update's presence.

Data Input Error Clarification:

Prompt: "The email format you provided seems off. Kindly verify and input again."

Interpretation: The beauty of this prompt lies in its precise clarity. It goes beyond a mere error alert, guiding the user to the exact problem area

Less-Than-Stellar Prompts: Missteps to Reflect Upon

Vague Error Alert:

Prompt: "Oops! Something's amiss."

Interpretation: Such generic declarations are more hindrance than help. Their vagueness leaves users in the lurch, leading to needless aggravation.

Dense Registration Guidance:

Prompt: "For a password, combine 8-16 characters, blend in uppercase and lowercase, mix in numerals, evade common terms, and toss in symbols like # or *."

Interpretation: Despite the noble intent of ensuring a strong password, the sheer volume of directives can intimidate and potentially repel prospective users.

Impersonal App Access Request:

Prompt: "App Y wishes to view your contacts."

Interpretation: Lacking in context and rationale, such a prompt can set off alarms. Users are left pondering the necessity of this access, raising potential privacy red flags.

Deciphering the Divide

The chasm between stellar and subpar prompts isn't confined to word choices—it mirrors the foundational approach:

User Emphasis: Exceptional prompts are invariably user-centric. They pre-empt user requirements, allay potential concerns, and strike the right information balance. Conversely, system-centric prompts can sow seeds of confusion or skepticism.

Directness Over Doubt: The primary mandate of a prompt is clarity in its message or action direction. Ambiguity can engender hesitation, making users rethink their ensuing moves or doubt system dependability.

Upholding User Sovereignty: Optimal prompts find equilibrium between user guidance and empowerment. Oversteering or under-explaining can come off as overbearing or neglectful.

Charting the Path for Prompt Crafting

Drawing wisdom from these practical insights, here's a blueprint for prompt strategy:

Foresee and Address: Adopt the user's lens. What might they seek? What apprehensions could surface?

Champion Brevity: Resist the allure of verbosity. Retain focus, ensuring the core message remains undiluted.

Evaluate and Adapt: Like any user-centric element, prompts merit evaluation. Elicit feedback, gauge user sentiment, and be nimble in refinement.

Wrapping Up

As pivotal cogs in the user interaction machinery, prompts wield considerable influence over user journeys. They can champion actions, simplify pathways, or avert missteps. Harnessing real-world examples—both triumphs and blunders—can chart the course for designing prompts that resonate, enlighten, and support. The ultimate aspiration is an elegant dance where system aspirations harmoniously intertwine with user desires, transforming each touchpoint into a user-centric dialogue.

Lessons learned from high-profile AI dialogue systems

As AI dialogue platforms have surged to the forefront, reshaping our interaction modalities, decision-making processes, and information access, their journeys offer rich learning avenues. High-caliber systems, from conversational bots to digital assistants, championed by both tech behemoths and emerging startups, present a spectrum of lessons in terms of design nuances, deployment strategies, and user engagement. Delving deep into these prominent instances can pave the way for refined future innovations.

1. The Pivotal Role of Contextual Comprehension

Highlight: Initial iterations of popular virtual assistants, including Alexa and Siri, occasionally grappled with deciphering user intention within extended dialogues.

Insight: Beyond processing standalone requests, the success of AI dialogue platforms hinges on their prowess in recognizing and recalling the broader dialogue context. This not only upholds continuity but also circumvents redundant information provisioning by users.

2. Navigating Ethical Concerns and Biases

Highlight: Microsoft's Tay, designed for Twitter interactions, was swiftly decommissioned post-launch due to its generation of inappropriate comments under user influence.

Insight: The integrity of AI dialogue platforms mirrors the quality and diversity of their training data. Rigorous dataset curation, along with implementing stringent checks, is quintessential to neutralize biases, deter potential misuse, and align the AI's responses with established societal values.

3. Bracing for Uncharted User Interactions

Highlight: Several chatbots have been caught off guard with unanticipated user inquiries or unconventional language usage.

Insight: Users invariably bring a palette of unexpected interactions to the table. Systems that adeptly manage these unpredictables, either with pertinent replies or candid non-understanding admissions, fare better. Instituting feedback loops from such engagements can bolster system resilience.

4. Upholding User Trust through Data Privacy

Highlight: Concerns have periodically arisen around virtual assistants inadvertently monitoring and archiving user conversations.

Insight: Absolute transparency in data handling, fortified security protocols, and granting users autonomy over their data are paramount. Trust, once compromised in the AI space, is arduous to reclaim.

5. The Delicate Equilibrium: Human-esque vs. Robotic

Highlight: Google's Duplex, renowned for executing phone tasks for users, faced initial criticism for not identifying as an AI during interactions.

Insight: While emulating human conversational intricacies augments AI user experience, it's equally vital to demarcate the AI's non-human essence. Both users and external interactors should be cognizant of the AI backdrop.

6. The Continuous Evolutionary Cycle

Highlight: Renowned AI platforms, from the GPT lineup to IBM's Watson, have seen manifold refinements based on real-world feedback.

Insight: Launching an AI dialogue tool marks the commencement of its evolutionary journey. Persistent monitoring, feedback assimilation, and cyclical improvements are instrumental in ensuring its progressive alignment with user expectations.

7. Crafting Transparent Boundaries

Highlight: Early users of chatbots and digital assistants often harbored lofty expectations, leading to subsequent disillusionment.

Insight: Demarcating the AI's operational boundaries helps steer user expectations. While positioning AI dialogue systems as groundbreaking is tempting, it's crucial to underscore their inherent limitations.

8. The Confluence of Diverse Expertise

Highlight: Elite dialogue systems are typically birthed from synergies between language experts, software architects, cognitive scholars, and domain specialists.

Insight: Constructing a sophisticated AI dialogue tool isn't just a coding endeavor. It's a mosaic of linguistic mastery, cultural insights, specialized knowledge, and an understanding of human cognition. Collaborative, cross-disciplinary endeavors invariably produce superior outcomes.

In Closing

The odyssey of AI dialogue platforms, marked by celebrated successes and instructive challenges, offers a repository of insights. As we stand on the cusp of further technological evolution, these distilled lessons can guide us towards crafting systems that are technologically robust, ethically aligned, and user-oriented.

Success stories of businesses leveraging prompt engineering

The innovative domain of prompt engineering skillfully marries the nuances of designing inputs to derive meaningful AI responses with the rigorous methodologies of machine learning optimization. The commercial landscape has astutely discerned its value, harnessing it for enriched user touchpoints, fortified decision frameworks, and beyond. Some distinct business episodes vividly demonstrate the profound influence of this craft.

1. Digital Retail Outlets: Curating Bespoke User Journeys

A foremost online shopping platform discerned that fostering a deeply individualized browsing experience was pivotal for customer loyalty. Capitalizing on prompt engineering, they finetuned their AI system to generate exacting product suggestions. This meticulous input design led to a remarkable 15% surge in user activity and a consequent boost in transaction rates.

2. Banking Sector: Bolstering Fraud Identification

A prestigious global banking entity aimed to curtail unauthorized actions across its vast transactional matrix. While traditional methodologies were proficient, they had inherent constraints. Embracing prompt engineering, the institution sculpted inputs to derive more intricate outputs, culminating in a 20% enhancement in pinpointing irregular transactions and safeguarding countless user accounts.

3. Medical Domain: Elevating Diagnostics and Patient Rapport

Within healthcare, the ramifications of prompt engineering have been transformative. An international health service incorporated it into its diagnostic AI frameworks. By calibrating the prompts rooted in distinct patient narratives, the AI provided sharper diagnostic insights. Simultaneously, the patient-facing AI interfaces, equipped with engineered prompts, conversed with heightened sensitivity, crafting a more comprehensive care experience.

4. Entertainment Sphere: Personalized Content Suggestions

A media streaming giant, catering to audiences worldwide, was challenged with aligning content choices to diverse viewer preferences. By embracing prompt engineering, they redefined their AI-driven content suggestions. This nuanced approach led to a more adaptive recommendation engine, signified by a sustained user engagement and diminished search durations.

5. Client Support: Enhancing Query Resolutions

Customer interactions remain a vital business interface, with AI-assisted mechanisms gaining traction. A top-tier software entity utilized prompt engineering to elevate its support mechanisms. Tailoring prompts anchored in user interactions and feedback, the digital assistant displayed increased proficiency in addressing concerns, culminating in amplified user appreciation.

6. Promotional Realm: Fine-tuning Advertisement Strategies

In the bustling digital marketing arena, targeted precision is paramount. A dominant advertising enterprise incorporated prompt engineering to refine its AI-centric ad strategies. By honing input prompts aligned with user demographics and digital footprints, optimal advertisement placements were identified, heralding a significant uptick in user engagement.

7. Distribution Networks: Streamlined Transit Plans

A leading global dispatch entity, overseeing an expansive vehicular fleet, pivoted towards prompt engineering to refine its AI-driven route suggestions. Inputs crafted with real-time navigational data, atmospheric conditions, and delivery urgencies empowered the AI to chart out superior pathways, culminating in expedited deliveries and operational savings.

8. Innovation Hubs: Swift Knowledge Procurement

Global corporate R&D divisions are increasingly reliant on AI for data extraction. A tech titan, through adept prompt engineering, streamlined its queries to their informational AI system. This facilitated rapid and pertinent data aggregation, fostering research velocity and nurturing groundbreaking solutions.

Final Reflections

These compelling tales emphasize the instrumental role of prompt engineering in today's dynamic business environment. As AI's influence extends across myriad sectors, the precision of our dialogues with these systems becomes crucial. The aforementioned narratives not only encapsulate the real-world advantages businesses can harness but also signal a transformative phase where AI interfaces align symbiotically with human aspirations, all propelled by the artistry of prompt engineering.

Chapter Eleven

The Future of Prompt Engineering

Predictions and trends for the next decade

The trajectory of technological advancement over the next decade promises profound shifts in both global landscapes and individual lifestyles. As we stand on the cusp of myriad breakthroughs, ranging from the melding of the virtual and real to the leap into quantum realms, it's essential to project and understand the potential trends that may shape the 2030s.

1. Quantum Computing Breaks New Ground

Classical computers, albeit powerful, have limitations rooted in their binary core. Quantum computers, operating on qubits, are positioned to overcome these. By the 2030s, the practical applications of quantum machines might outpace traditional systems, driving innovations in fields such as cryptography, pharmaceuticals, and advanced materials.

2. The Seamless Confluence of Real and Digital Worlds

The boundary separating our physical existence from the digital one is becoming increasingly porous. Technologies like Augmented Reality (AR) and Virtual Reality (VR) will intertwine with our daily routines, from professional engagements to leisure activities. This amalgamation will lead to holistic mixed reality platforms, revolutionizing sectors including education, healthcare, and tourism.

3. AI's Ubiquitous Role in Decision Making

The coming decade will see AI's influence extend across varied sectors, evolving into an omnipresent digital partner. As machine learning algorithms become sophisticated, they'll play pivotal roles in areas from medical diagnostics to financial planning. This widespread integration will necessitate stringent ethical checks and transparency measures.

4. A New Era in Transportation

Autonomous vehicles won't just be confined to roads. The future might see the skies above our cities dotted with drone taxis, while rapid transit solutions, inspired by hyperloop models, could redefine terrestrial travel by connecting cities efficiently and sustainably.

5. Urban Centers as Intelligent Entities

Cities of the future will evolve into holistic, interconnected smart systems. Leveraging 6G networks and sophisticated IoT setups, they will autonomously manage aspects ranging from public health and safety to infrastructure maintenance. Green technologies and sustainable practices will underpin urban development.

6. Tailored Healthcare through Biotech Innovations

The nexus of biotechnology will reshape healthcare, offering tailor-made treatments. Advanced genetic interventions, leveraging tools like CRISPR, might provide cures for previously untreatable conditions. Remote healthcare interactions, powered by telemedicine, will become commonplace.

7. Emphasis on Circular Economic Models

Environmental consciousness will spearhead shifts in industrial practices. The emphasis will be on minimal waste and maximal resource utilization. Renewable energy sources will dominate power generation, while novel solutions like cellular agriculture and vertical farms could overhaul the agricultural sector.

8. Evolving Financial Paradigms

Blockchain's ripple effect on global financial systems will continue, with decentralized finance (DeFi) taking center stage. Conventional banking mechanisms will likely intertwine with blockchain platforms, leading to hybrid financial models characterized by increased transparency and robustness.

9. Cybersecurity's Ever-evolving Landscape

The increasing valuation of digital assets necessitates reinforced protective mechanisms. Advanced cybersecurity strategies, using AI for proactive threat identification and quantum methodologies for data protection, will be central.

10. Commercial Ventures in Outer Space

Space exploration will increasingly be steered by commercial entities alongside national programs. Recreational space travel could transition from concept to reality, and initiatives like asteroid excavation and lunar colonization may gain traction.

In Summation

The next decade is poised to be a period of unparalleled technological crescendos. While these trends bring excitement, they also demand agility and foresight. Balancing innovation with ethical considerations will be paramount to ensure a future that's both progressive and principled.

The integration of augmented reality, virtual reality, and AI

In our swiftly evolving digital landscape, progress isn't just about one technology rising independently, but often a blend of multiple technologies coming together. The exciting intersection of Augmented Reality (AR), Virtual Reality (VR), and Artificial Intelligence (AI) is setting the stage for a revolution in the way we engage with and within digital arenas.

Augmented Reality (AR): Enriching the Real World

Simply put, AR infuses digital information into our actual environment, enabling users to have an enhanced real-world experience. Using gadgets like AR glasses, tablets, and smartphones, individuals can perceive holographic projections, graphical displays, and data superimposed on their tangible surroundings.

Virtual Reality (VR): A Dive into Digital Realms

Contrastingly, VR offers a simulated environment where users can enter and engage entirely within these digital worlds through immersive equipment like VR headsets.

AI: The Powerhouse Behind the Scenes

Serving as the foundation for refining AR and VR, AI offers a range of sophisticated applications from deep learning to neural computations, ensuring that digital experiences are intuitive, adjustable, and reactive.

Where They Meet and Elevate Each Other

1. Tailored Digital Interactions:

AI's capability to process information ensures that AR and VR are molded to fit each user. Be it AR-guided shopping experiences suggesting items based on user behavior, or VR educational modules that evolve according to a learner's pace, AI guarantees personalized engagement.

2. Intelligent Recognition and Engagement:

AR/VR systems, when combined with AI, can better interpret and adapt to their settings. In an AR setup, apps might recognize real-world items and offer relevant digital insights. In VR, AI could regulate the behavior of virtual characters based on user inputs, leading to dynamic experiences.

3. Lifelike Simulations through AI:

Deep learning models can generate incredibly detailed graphics, movements, and shadows in VR settings. Similarly, in AR, facial tracking and movement capture become more refined, ensuring a smooth fusion of digital elements with the real world.

4. Informed Decision Processes:

In professional arenas, AR combined with AI can offer real-time guidance. Imagine technicians repairing intricate equipment with AR displaying necessary data and AI providing problem-solving pathways based on predictive analysis.

5. Evolving Learning Environments:

Educational setups can benefit from the trio, crafting platforms that gauge a student's understanding instantly. A VR chemistry class about molecular structures might change its difficulty based on the learner's responses, all underlined by AI's analytical capabilities.

Navigating the Challenges

Yet, the union of AR, VR, and AI poses certain challenges:

1. Safeguarding User Data:

Given AI's role in processing immense datasets to hone AR/VR experiences, concerns arise around potential data abuse, security breaches, and the ethical dimensions of continuous user surveillance.

2. Technical Hurdles:

Delivering top-tier VR and AR experiences requires considerable computational resources. Even with AI's optimization strategies, there's a pressing demand for high-performance, lag-free gadgets.

3. Crafting Content:

Building immersive and adaptive AR/VR content that integrates AI requires multidisciplinary expertise. Given the emerging nature of this integrated domain, content creators face a significant learning journey.

4. Health Considerations:

Long durations in AR or VR environments might cause discomfort or health issues for users. When fusing AI, which could amplify the intensity of these experiences, a focus on user-centric designs becomes paramount.

Wrapping Up

As AR, VR, and AI become more intertwined, they're setting the course for a future where our digital and tangible experiences are more integrated than we ever imagined. This union promises groundbreaking applications across many sectors but also calls for strategies that weigh technical, ethical, and human-centric factors. The synergy of these technologies will undoubtedly redefine our interaction paradigms and reshape our worldview.

Potential societal impacts and challenges

The relentless march of technology has ushered in a myriad of transformative changes, reshaping the way we perceive and engage with our world. Like every transformative epoch, the digital, bioengineering, and cognitive revolutions come bearing both boons and dilemmas, influencing societal norms, economic structures, and moral codes. This piece delves into the multifaceted societal ramifications and challenges germinating from these technological advances.

1. Societal Ramifications:

Economic Shifts:

The rise of automation, artificial intelligence, and data-driven processes promises to redefine industries and work paradigms. While there's potential for job redundancy in certain arenas, a plethora of unique job roles also beckon, necessitating a resilient and ever-evolving workforce.

Global Linkages:

The ubiquity of internet access and sophisticated communication mediums is making the world a closer-knit community. This heightened connectivity stimulates cultural intermingling, widens market reach, and has become a fulcrum for social advocacy spanning local to global scales.

Healthcare Evolution:

Emerging technologies like telemedicine, genomics, and AI-infused diagnostics herald an era of personalized and streamlined healthcare. Such innovations hint at superior disease prevention, longer life spans, and a democratization of health resources.

Eco-conscious Innovations:

Tech-driven solutions, from renewable energy systems to advanced waste management methods, hold the promise of mitigating environmental challenges and driving sustainable growth trajectories.

Educational Innovations:

The rise of digital classrooms, AI-aided learning platforms, and online knowledge repositories augur a more inclusive, individualized, and accessible educational landscape.

2. Societal Hurdles:

Technological Disparities:

Despite the promise of a universal digital age, gaps in technological accessibility can intensify existing inequalities. Communities bereft of the means or know-how to capitalize on these advancements risk being marginalized.

Data Security Concerns:

Our entwined existence with smart technologies raises alarms about personal data sanctity. Vulnerabilities to data misuse, illicit surveillance, and cyber incursions are pressing issues in this interconnected era.

Moral Quandaries:

Cutting-edge technologies, be it genetic modifications or AI-led surveillance tools, meander into ethically gray zones. The task before societies is to strike a balance between innovation and its moral ramifications.

Digital Well-being:

The omnipresence of digital interfaces has ripple effects on mental health. From the strain of constant online engagements to the perils of digital isolationism and cyber harassment, the challenges are multifaceted.

Workforce Dynamics:

While tech evolutions birth new vocational arenas, they also render certain roles obsolete. The imperative is to foster agility and resilience, ensuring transitional support and re-skilling avenues for the impacted populace.

Techno-political Dynamics:

Technological prowess has entwined with global geopolitics. Concerns spanning cyber threats, digital espionage, and the competitive quest for tech supremacy add intricate layers to international diplomacy and strategic posturing.

To Conclude

At this crossroad of sweeping societal metamorphosis steered by tech innovations, a judicious blend of optimism and vigilance is warranted. By championing equitable access, harnessing technology's vast potential, and preemptively addressing emergent challenges, societies can craft a harmonious future, synergistically aligning technological progress with human aspirations.

Chapter Twelve

Building a Career in Prompt Engineering

Key skills and qualifications required

Navigating the ever-evolving professional environment of today, marked by relentless technological advances and shifts in industry standards, necessitates a broad spectrum of qualifications and skill sets. As the contours of established professions morph and new fields emerge, there's a marked focus on varied expertise. This exploration delves into the contemporary competencies that are now in high demand.

1. Mastery of the Digital Realm:

Basic Digital Know-how: In our digital-first era, familiarity with software, online platforms, and digital tools is essential. From mastering productivity software suites to understanding diverse operating systems, these are non-negotiable essentials.

Understanding Cyber Risks: The rise in cyber threats demands knowledge about cybersecurity basics, from creating strong passwords to recognizing phishing scams.

Software Development Skills: The ability to develop, interpret, and adjust software has growing significance, finding relevance in various sectors beyond the traditional tech space.

2. Aptitude for Data:

Data Interpretation: As organizational strategies lean on data, the ability to gather, analyze, and decipher data becomes essential. Proficiency in analytical tools like Python, R, and visualization platforms like Tableau is beneficial.

Foundations of AI and ML: Basic knowledge of artificial intelligence structures, machine learning processes, and related concepts are distinguishing skills in sectors ranging from health to finance.

3. Interpersonal Abilities:

Clear Communication: The skill to articulate concepts, relay feedback, and share insights, both orally and in writing, is of paramount importance.

Rational Analysis: In an era flooded with information, the capacity to objectively evaluate data, consider different perspectives, and formulate informed decisions is vital.

Flexibility: Rapid changes call for a mindset of perpetual learning and an ability to adapt, ensuring continued relevance in shifting contexts.

Cooperative Dynamics: Diverse work settings and interdisciplinary ventures highlight the need to collaborate efficiently with peers from various disciplines.

4. Sector-specific Credentials:

Industry-specific Endorsements: Depending on the chosen field, specialized certifications can enhance one's professional standing. Consider credentials like PMP in project oversight, CEH in cybersecurity, or CFA in the financial sector.

Higher Educational Pursuits: Specialized roles often require deep academic commitment, be it an MBA for corporate insights, MS for technical specialization, or Ph.D. for research-centric positions.

5. Sustainability-focused Expertise:

Environmental Analysis: With businesses becoming more eco-conscious, gauging the ecological implications of activities is critical.

Skills in Green Energy: Expertise in conceptualizing, executing, or maintaining green energy solutions, like solar grids or wind energy setups, are in the spotlight.

6. Design Thinking and User Orientation:

Crafting User Journeys: The move towards digital means there's a growing importance in designing intuitive user interfaces and enhancing user engagement.

Conceptual Design Skills: Mastery in tools such as Adobe XD, Figma, or Sketch for visualizing digital solutions is sought after.

7. Strategic Oversight and Efficiency:

Project Visualization: Charting out project pathways, ensuring optimal resource use, and foreseeing potential challenges are keys to effective management.

Efficient Tasking: Balancing varied assignments, setting task priorities, and adhering to schedules elevate individual and organizational efficiency.

Building Relationships: Maintaining and fostering ties with diverse project stakeholders, from clients to suppliers, is central to achieving project objectives

8. Global Communication Skills:

Language Proficiency: Being multilingual is an asset in a globally connected workplace, enhancing outreach and understanding.

Appreciation of Cultural Diversities: Engaging in multi-cultural environments requires an awareness of and respect for diverse cultural practices and etiquettes.

To Conclude

The professional world of today demands a harmonious blend of tech-savviness, cognitive strength, and people skills. While some expertise is universally relevant, some cater to specific sectors. To successfully traverse this dynamic scenario, one needs to be open to ongoing learning, ready to adapt, and willing to embrace a spectrum of knowledge areas. Armed with the right skills and qualifications, the opportunities for innovation, growth, and meaningful contributions are limitless.

Potential career paths and job roles

As the world undergoes rapid technological and global shifts, the spectrum of professional opportunities has expanded, presenting a rich tapestry of career paths and roles. This diversification of job profiles is significant for both upcoming professionals and employers. Here's a detailed look into this evolving world.

1. The Digital Tech Revolution:

Application Engineer: At the heart of our digital age, these experts design, create, and sustain software tools and platforms that power today's businesses.

Analytics Specialist: Utilizing the strength of massive datasets, these experts extract insights that shape business trajectories and refine decisions.

Information Security Expert: With the digital realm being continuously threatened, these individuals protect systems, ensuring data remains uncompromised.

Deployment Specialist: They work to smoothen software rollouts, emphasizing streamlined processes and system automation.

2. Advances in Medicine and Biosciences:

Bioengineer: Working where biology meets technology, bioengineers spearhead breakthroughs across medicine, farming, and ecological solutions.

Medical Research Coordinator: They helm the planning, execution, and evaluation of clinical studies, paving the way for medical advancements.

Genomic Advisor: As individualized healthcare gains traction, these professionals guide individuals on genetic findings and their health implications.

3. Green Energy and Ecological Innovation:

Energy Solutions Architect: Essential in our transition towards cleaner energy sources, they develop and fine-tune energy conservation techniques.

Eco-Consultant: These experts guide corporations on ecological best practices, synergizing business ambitions with environmental conservation.

Green Initiatives Director: They embed eco-conscious strategies into organizational operations, products, and growth plans.

4. Financial Technologies and Modern Banking:

Distributed Ledger Developer: They're at the forefront of reshaping traditional finance by creating and maintaining decentralized digital databases, bolstering transparency and resilience.

Financial Modeler: Leveraging math and statistical tools, these experts calibrate financial outcomes and guide investment trajectories.

Wealth Strategist: They counsel both individuals and entities, crafting financial roadmaps that encompass investments to retirement goals.

5. Evolving Media and Artistic Domains:

Interaction Designer: Concentrating on user journeys, they refine interactions within digital environments, elevating user contentment and involvement.

Digital Media Creator: Using advanced tools, they produce a mix of visual and auditory elements, spanning animations, visuals, and sound compositions.

Publication Director: They don't just produce content; they strategically ascertain the ideal content type, timing, and distribution channels for maximum audience connection.

6. Aerospace and Space Exploration:

Aviation Systems Designer: Spearheading aerial and space innovation, they conceptualize and create airborne vehicles, ensuring operational excellence and safety parameters.

Exobiology Researcher: Delving into cosmic mysteries, they investigate life possibilities beyond our planet, studying extraterrestrial environments and life indicators.

Orbital Data Specialist: By analyzing data from celestial instruments, they cater to varied sectors, from weather forecasting to global communication.

7. Digital Education and Learning Platforms:

E-Learning Architect: Combining teaching principles with tech, they draft impactful digital learning paths, from online courses to immersive simulations.

Tech Integration Educator: They introduce and embed technological tools in learning environments, training teachers and shaping institutional tech strategies.

8. Social Dynamics and Worldwide Diplomacy:

Metro Development Expert: Addressing urban growth challenges, they envision urban designs that reconcile progress, sustainability, and resident welfare.

Global Affairs Researcher: They analyze and interpret global political movements, advising on policies to nurture alliances and uphold national agendas.

9. Agriculture and Tech-driven Farming:

Agro-Tech Specialist: By employing technologies from aerial devices to connected devices, they refine farming techniques, boosting productivity and ecological harmony.

FarmTech Innovator: They ideate and rollout agricultural innovations, from intelligent watering systems to early disease detection tools.

In Summary:

The vast array of career paths and roles in the current professional arena underscores the symbiosis of technology, societal imperatives, and pioneering thought. For career enthusiasts, marrying personal passion with market needs and staying receptive to new trends is paramount. Organizations, too, should recognize and cultivate environments conducive to such roles, positioning themselves strongly for a dynamic future.

Tips for aspiring prompt engineers

The dynamic world of artificial intelligence (AI) offers a plethora of avenues for professionals eager to establish a niche. Among the various roles surfacing, the position of 'Prompt Engineer' has caught the industry's eye. This role pivots around crafting, refining, and optimizing prompts for AI dialogue mechanisms, acting as a linchpin between intricate AI mechanics and nuanced human interaction. For those intrigued by this specialized vocation, here's a distilled list of pointers to guide your journey.

1. Champion Lifelong Learning:

The AI sphere is in perpetual motion. Staying updated with emerging technologies, new techniques, and methodologies is more than just beneficial – it's a necessity. Delve into specialized literature, virtual tutorials, and hands-on sessions to deepen and update your expertise.

2. Fine-tune Your Linguistic Acumen:

Prompt engineering is deeply rooted in language. Dive into the depths of semantics, syntax, and various aspects of linguistic studies. Opt for structured courses in linguistics or human cognition to broaden your horizon.

3. Sharpen Your Technical Edge:

Beyond linguistic prowess, the realm of prompt engineering requires a sound technical foundation. Acquainting oneself with coding languages like Python and understanding AI ecosystems will stand you in good stead.

4. Nurture Inquisitiveness and Innovative Thinking:

The key to exceptional prompt crafting lies in thinking unconventionally and predicting diverse user inputs. Keep the flame of inquisitiveness alive and consistently challenge conventional wisdom.

5. Engross Yourself in Practical Endeavors:

While theoretical knowledge is foundational, its practical application cements understanding. Embark on tangible projects, irrespective of their scale, to gain practical insights and beef up your professional showcase.

6. Adopt a User-first Mindset:

The end user is your North Star. Tailor prompts to align with user expectations, accounting for their possible queries, cultural undertones, and linguistic comfort.

7. Tackle Biases Head-on:

AI interfaces, by design or accident, can mirror societal biases. Arm yourself with the expertise and tools to identify and counteract such latent biases in prompt design.

8. Forge Collaborative Bonds:

Diverse interactions breed fresh insights. Make your presence felt at AI symposiums, web workshops, and online AI forums. Such engagements not only facilitate continuous learning but also pave the way for potential job prospects and synergistic ventures.

9. Seek Wise Counsel:

A guiding hand can be transformative in one's professional journey. Find seasoned professionals who've etched a mark in this niche and are receptive to guiding budding talent.

10. Cultivate Flexibility and Tenacity:

With AI's relentless pace, the landscape can sometimes feel daunting. Obsolescence is a real threat, and new hurdles are par for the course. Embrace change, remain tenacious, and be ready to recalibrate your strategies.

11. Uphold Ethical Practices:

Beyond inherent biases, it's crucial for prompt engineers to be aware of the broader ethical ramifications of their work. Whether it revolves around safeguarding user data or creating transparent prompts, ethics should always be paramount.

12. Straddle the Automation-Human Interface:

While AI thrives on automation, discerning when to defer to human discretion remains vital. Recognize that AI might not have all the answers, and occasional human oversight could be the missing piece.

13. Actively Seek Constructive Criticism:

Feedback is the crucible for refinement. Regularly solicit perspectives on your work from users, peers, and industry experts. Use this input as a launchpad for continual evolution.

14. Probe Specialized Domains:

As you immerse in prompt engineering, certain segments may resonate more. Delving deeper into these specialized arenas can amplify your market value.

15. Stay Abreast of Regulatory Shifts:

With AI's ubiquitous integration in daily life, governing bodies are setting the rulebook. A keen understanding of these evolving norms, especially for dialogue systems, is indispensable.

To Sum Up:

Stepping into the shoes of a prompt engineer is exhilarating, with countless opportunities to redefine AI-human dialogues. With the right skill set, a user-centric vision, and an adaptive mindset, budding prompt engineers can not only find their groove but truly thrive in this specialized sphere.

Chapter Thirteen

Community and Further Resources

Connecting with the global community of prompt engineers

The modern tech landscape has illuminated the significance of prompt engineers. These experts, pivotal in shaping, fine-tuning, and enhancing prompts for AI dialogue mechanisms, act as the bridge between intricate AI operations and human-focused interaction. As the requirement for this specialized skill grows, it's vital for these engineers to network, team up, and exchange expertise on an international scale. Immersing oneself in this expansive community can lead to not only personal growth but also to the advancement of the industry as a whole.

Gaining a Grip on the Global Scene

Before actively joining the global discourse, one needs to first grasp the diverse facets of prompt engineering on an international scale. Even though some core tenets remain consistent, differences in culture, language, and technology introduce unique challenges and prospects. By recognizing these disparities, prompt engineers can cater more adeptly to global users.

Blueprint for Global Interaction

Engage in World-renowned Events: Major conferences and seminars, whether in-person or online, offer golden opportunities for peer interaction. Such events present a chance to delve into the latest research, technological strides, and best practices from various regions.

Active Online Forum Participation: Platforms such as community boards, specialized groups, and industry-specific networks can be instrumental in fostering continuous learning and interaction. These spaces encourage real-time exchanges, problem-solving, and can spawn potential global collaborations.

Team Up for International Initiatives: Partnering with peers from diverse backgrounds can enhance one's adaptability to global demands. Such collaborations highlight the importance of understanding cultural and linguistic subtleties to create universally applicable AI systems.

Undertake Diverse Communication Training: Programs that focus on global communication can refine prompt engineers' abilities to better engage with international colleagues. Such sessions often delve deep into cultural interactions, non-verbal communication patterns, and linguistic nuances.

Harness Worldwide Knowledge Platforms: Digital libraries, scholarly databases, and other online resources offer insights from experts around the world. Regular interaction with these resources ensures professionals remain at the forefront of industry trends and share their expertise with a wider audience.

Foster Mentorships: Emerging professionals can immensely benefit from guidance provided by experienced peers with a global perspective. On the flip side, seasoned experts can aid fresh talent, promoting a culture of shared growth.

Join International Research Endeavors: Projects, especially those under global banners, benefit from diverse expert input. Engaging in these projects allows prompt engineers to explore new areas and align with international standards.

Stay Updated on Global AI Norms: As AI integrates deeper into our routines, nations are crafting specific regulations around these systems. Awareness of these standards aids prompt engineers in designing globally compliant solutions.

Potential Hurdles and Solutions

Engaging on a global scale offers its set of challenges. Differences in time zones, language, and technology can pose obstacles. Yet, with innovative tools, cloud solutions, and instant translation features, these challenges are surmountable.

Moreover, it's imperative for prompt engineers to navigate global engagements with an ethical compass. It's essential to uphold user confidentiality, data protection measures, and respect for intellectual property. Also, it's crucial to approach global interactions with cultural sensitivity, ensuring AI systems remain inclusive and devoid of inadvertent biases.

Wrapping Up

In an era where tech breakthroughs transcend geographical barriers, professionals, including prompt engineers, should seek to broaden their perspectives. By networking with the global community, they can gain access to a vast pool of knowledge, diverse viewpoints, and groundbreaking approaches. This not only fuels personal progression but also strengthens the collective prowess and reach of the prompt engineering domain.

Conferences, workshops, and forums to attend

In the swiftly advancing realm of technology, continuous learning is of the essence. A powerful way for industry professionals to stay current with the latest methodologies, advancements, and practices is by participating in recognized conferences, workshops, and forums. For those working in areas like AI, prompt engineering, and related disciplines, a diverse range of premier events beckon on the international stage.

Premier Conferences

NeurIPS (Conference on Neural Information Processing Systems): Positioned as a leading gathering in machine learning, NeurIPS regularly showcases a distinguished list of global thought leaders. Delegates can anticipate detailed explorations into new research discoveries, algorithmic progress, and pioneering applications.

ICLR (International Conference on Learning Representations): Dedicated to representation learning, ICLR stands as a beacon for those keen on delving into novel deep learning strategies. With its rigorous paper acceptance process, the conference ensures a rich menu of discussions and insights.

AAAI (Association for the Advancement of Artificial Intelligence) Conference: As a touchstone event for the AI community, AAAI offers a panoramic snapshot of the discipline's milestones. With themes spanning robotics to cognitive understanding, it paints a vivid picture of AI's current landscape and potential future.

Specialized Workshops

OpenAI Workshops: Given OpenAI's pivotal role in shaping AI's direction and deployment, their curated workshops touch upon emergent topics. Centered on ethics, real-world viability, and resilience, these gatherings are indispensable for prompt engineering enthusiasts and others.

Deep Learning Summer School: Designed for those eager to reinforce their base knowledge and gain applied expertise, this summer school provides an immersive experience. Its blend of interactive discourse, hands-on labs, and expert perspectives promises enrichment.

Reinforcement Learning Workshops: As reinforcement learning gathers momentum, workshops focusing on this area are seeing heightened interest. Participants can look forward to a mix of intensive training, real-world cases, and applicative insights.

Dynamic Forums

AI Alignment Forum: With AI systems scaling new complexities, harmonizing their outputs with human ideals is a pressing concern. This collaborative space is dedicated to unpicking alignment challenges, pondering ethical dimensions, and brainstorming possible routes forward.

AI Ethics Forum: Amidst rising apprehensions about AI's societal footprint, this forum stands as a melting pot for cross-disciplinary dialogue. Central discussions hover around ensuring fairness, establishing accountability, amplifying transparency, and the overarching quest of orienting AI for the collective good.

Prompt Engineering Communities: Recognizing the specialized domain of prompt engineering, dedicated online communities have emerged. Platforms such as Reddit or Stack Exchange host these forums, offering rich repositories of advice, shared best practices, and mutual support.

Optimizing the Experience at Conferences and Workshops

It's not enough to just be present at these events; a proactive stance is pivotal. Before the event:

Outline Objectives: Identify clear goals, whether that's mastering a technique, forging connections, or seeking answers to a particular dilemma.

Engage with Pre-Event Offerings: Many forums offer tutorials, preparatory webinars, or suggested readings. Engaging with these can provide a foundational advantage.

During the event:

Dive In: From posing queries, immersing in hands-on sessions, or initiating dialogues during intervals, a proactive approach can expand horizons and unlock prospects.

Capture Insights: In the face of the torrent of knowledge typical of these events, jotting down key takeaways can aid recall and future consultation.

After the event:

Reflect and Disseminate: Ponder over the gained insights, share them with colleagues or through blog posts, thereby reinforcing the learning and establishing thought leadership.

Foster Connections: Networking shouldn't conclude with the event's end. Maintaining regular contact with new acquaintances, diving into post-event digital spaces, or collaborating on shared ventures can be the genesis of long-term partnerships.

Wrapping Up

With the dynamic nature of AI and prompt engineering, lifelong learning is non-negotiable. Conferences, workshops, and forums are invaluable avenues for this journey. By meticulously choosing which events to attend and harnessing their offerings, professionals can ensure they are always a step ahead, guiding the tech world's evolution.

Recommended reading, courses, and online resources

Navigating the sophisticated domain of artificial intelligence and prompt engineering mandates a strong commitment to continuous education. To assist in this endeavor, a diverse range of books, online courses, and digital platforms have been assembled to enrich your understanding. Here's a comprehensive guide tailored to deepen your insights, stimulate innovative thought, and refine your proficiency.

Essential Literature

"Artificial Intelligence: A Modern Approach" by Stuart Russell and Peter Norvig: Recognized for its excellence, this book provides a robust introduction to AI's core principles, paired with insightful examples and thorough discussions.

"Deep Learning" by Ian Goodfellow, Yoshua Bengio, and Aaron Courville: Distinguished in its field, this text meticulously navigates the realm of deep learning, from foundational aspects to advanced explorations.

"Pattern Recognition and Machine Learning" by Christopher Bishop: An exceptional blend of theory and application, Bishop's work is a cornerstone for those keen on deciphering the nuances of machine learning.

"Human Compatible: Artificial Intelligence and the Problem of Control" by Stuart Russell: Moving beyond mere technicalities, this book offers a profound look into the broader implications of AI on society and ethics.

Noteworthy Courses

Deep Learning Specialization on Coursera (by Andrew Ng): Led by AI luminary, Andrew Ng, this series demystifies concepts ranging from neural networks to applied deep learning.

MIT's Introduction to Deep Learning: Accessible via MIT OpenCourseWare, this offering instills a strong foundation in deep learning, complemented by practical tasks and compelling case studies.

Fast.ai's Practical Deep Learning for Coders: This course is geared towards the practical side of deep learning, equipping learners with the skills to design and implement their models.

Stanford University's Machine Learning (by Andrew Ng on Coursera): A comprehensive introduction to facets of machine learning, from foundational principles to pattern recognition.

Digital Resource Hubs

ArXiv: An abundant archive of preprints from varied disciplines, offering a wealth of fresh insights and research findings for AI aficionados.

Distill: This platform excels at translating complex academic content into accessible, visually engaging narratives.

Towards Data Science: Situated on Medium, this hub serves up a diverse mix of pieces on AI, data science, and machine learning, penned by both seasoned experts and fresh voices.

OpenAI: Renowned in the AI space, OpenAI's wide-ranging materials, from in-depth research to tutorials, are essential for anyone serious about prompt engineering.

Engaging Multimedia Content

The AI Podcast (by NVIDIA): Delve deep into AI's multifaceted world through discussions with top industry figures and innovators.

Lex Fridman's Podcast: Engaging conversations with leading minds in AI and related areas make this series both informative and stimulating.

Two Minute Papers: This YouTube series offers succinct overviews of intricate research topics, making it an ideal pick for time-pressed enthusiasts.

To Summarize

The landscape of AI and prompt engineering is ever-shifting, and staying informed is paramount. While this compilation is by no means all-encompassing, it offers a solid foundation or next step. By engaging with these resources, both newcomers and established professionals can ensure they remain at the forefront of the discipline, poised to influence its ongoing evolution.

Conclusion

Recap of the major themes and takeaways

Upon revisiting the vast expanse of artificial intelligence (AI) and its related domains, we can identify several salient themes and vital lessons. This synthesis strives to coalesce these pivotal points, offering an integrated summation set within a comprehensive context.

1. The Rapid Progression and Dual Facets of AI

Over recent years, AI has shifted from being a budding concept to a foundational element in our technological realm. This dramatic evolution is a source of both wonder and contemplation. While AI mechanisms, spanning from language processing to data-driven predictions, have introduced innovative solutions, they've also raised pertinent ethical and societal issues.

Lesson: Harnessing the capabilities of AI mandates a judicious approach where groundbreaking developments are tempered with ethical and responsible practices.

2. Delving Deep into Prompt Engineering

The intricate task of prompt engineering highlighted the nuanced balance of directing AI interactions. Effective prompting isn't solely about explicit directives; it involves grasping the AI's foundational models, anticipating user interactions, and navigating the broader operational context.

Lesson: The realm of prompt engineering epitomizes the harmonization of tech-savviness with user-centric methodologies, accentuating the importance of a multidisciplinary approach.

3. Confronting and Mitigating AI Biases

The issue of ingrained bias in AI, whether linked to cultural, gender, or other aspects, is a topic of significant concern. Our discussions underscored the role of tech specialists, institutions, and community stakeholders in diligently combating these biases, ensuring the creation of just and balanced AI tools.

Lesson: Pursuing unbiased AI is not merely a technical endeavor; it's a societal commitment that requires broad-based collaboration.

4. AI's Symbiotic Relationship with AR and VR

Merging AI with augmented (AR) and virtual realities (VR) represents a pivotal phase in offering holistic, responsive user experiences. This combination opens up avenues for revolutionary applications across sectors like healthcare and education.

Lesson: AI's potential is magnified when integrated with other groundbreaking technologies, setting the stage for integrated platforms that redefine digital interactions.

5. Championing Data Privacy and Safeguarding User Information

With AI's increasing presence and the digitization of services, data protection concerns are more pronounced than ever. It's essential to find a middle ground between harnessing data insights and preserving user confidentiality.

Lesson: The responsibility of data protection is a collective one, encompassing service vendors, users, regulators, and the tech community at large.

6. The Imperative of Ongoing Adaptation and Growth

Given technology's fluid nature, an unwavering commitment to continuous learning is crucial. With the emergence of new methodologies and paradigm shifts, staying informed and agile is essential for both professionals and organizations.

Lesson: In the ever-evolving AI landscape, resilience and an inclination for constant learning are pivotal for sustained success.

7. Navigating the Broad Impact of AI on Society

AI's sweeping influence on various societal facets, from the economy to cultural nuances, is profound. While it promises transformative advantages, it also presents challenges like job realignment and potential privacy intrusions.

Lesson: Guiding AI's societal trajectory towards beneficial outcomes requires proactive strategies, inclusive policies, and a united effort to employ technology for societal advancement.

Wrapping Up

Our exploration of AI's multifaceted dimensions has shed light on its potential, intricacies, and associated challenges. Moving forward, it's clear that maximizing AI's benefits is a journey filled with hurdles. It demands mutual collaboration, ethical foresight, technical expertise, and an unyielding focus on human-centric innovation.

The ever-evolving nature of prompt engineering

The dynamic landscape of prompt engineering can be perceived as an amalgamation of technological advancements, linguistic insights, and the fluidity of user engagement. With AI seeing monumental shifts in recent times, the methodology and strategy behind crafting meaningful prompts have been no exception to this change. Delving into this metamorphosis provides insights into the current state of prompt engineering and forecasts its future trajectory.

In the beginning, prompts were largely simplistic, designed to be direct and often rigid. Early adaptations of voice assistants or automated helplines worked on a narrow spectrum of commands, faltering when users strayed from predefined inputs. However, with the blossoming of AI capabilities, the depth and breadth of prompts grew correspondingly.

One pivotal change in this domain has been the transition from systems that relied on strict rules to those that are adaptable and cognizant of context. Previously, each user query had to be painstakingly predicted and defined. Now, fortified with enhanced machine learning techniques, prompts can be more versatile, allowing systems to recognize and respond to a wider array of user statements. This progression has not only streamlined the process behind prompt engineering but also elevated the user's interaction experience.

The emergence of neural network architectures, especially transformer-based models like the GPT series, heralded a new era for prompt engineering. These models, ingrained with vast data, have the remarkable ability to emulate human-like text generation. For engineers in the field, this translates to the capability of guiding systems to yield outputs that are context-sensitive, layered, and occasionally, inventive. This advantage, however, comes with its set of challenges, primarily directing a system capable of endless response variations.

With technology platforms reaching global audiences, prompt engineering now grapples with cultural and linguistic intricacies. A prompt conceptualized for English-speaking users in the U.S. may not have the same impact or clarity for someone in China. Consequently, the craft of prompt engineering now integrates practices familiar to localization, ensuring AI systems maintain their efficacy across diverse demographic groups.

User feedback has progressively become a cornerstone for refining prompt engineering. Through interactions with AI-driven interfaces, users not only pinpoint glitches or inaccuracies but also illuminate unanticipated use scenarios and innovative interpretations. This feedback mechanism creates a cyclical enhancement process where real-world interactions continuously fine-tune and enrich the prompts.

Ethical concerns, too, have made their mark on the discipline. As AI models mirror the content inherent in their training data, they can unintentionally echo biases or yield outputs that are sensitive across various dimensions. Today's prompt engineers collaborate closely with specialists in ethics and cultural studies, guaranteeing that the crafted prompts are not just efficient but also ethically sound and culturally conscious.

Envisioning the future, prompt engineering promises to be a domain teeming with innovation. The fusion of multimodal frameworks—merging text, voice, imagery, and even gestures—foreshadows an era of more natural and comprehensive prompts. Furthermore, as technologies like augmented reality (AR) and virtual reality (VR) gain traction, prompt engineering will undergo further transformation, necessitating engineers to think beyond conventional paradigms.

To sum up, just as AI itself, prompt engineering is continually evolving. What started as the creation of uncomplicated, direct commands has matured into a field that intersects with linguistics, ethical considerations, and user-centric design. As we look forward, with AI becoming even more intertwined with our daily lives, the role and intricacies of prompt engineering are set to scale new heights. It demands professionals in the field to remain adaptable, perpetually updating their skills to navigate the rapid currents of technological and societal change.

Final words of inspiration for the budding prompt engineer

Navigating the world of prompt engineering offers a rich tapestry of experiences, bringing together the intricate ballet of human linguistics with the structured elegance of technology. For those poised on the cusp of this dynamic arena, a few motivating thoughts could prove instrumental in their pursuit.

Merging Creativity with Technology:

Prompt engineering is not merely a blend of codes and algorithms. It's the harmonization of tech prowess with the soulful cadence of human speech and sentiment. The true magic happens at this intersection. Allow the digital realm of binary codes to entwine with the vibrant human narrative. This will be the keystone of your pioneering contributions.

Stay Agile Amidst Change:

The only constant in the tech world is change. What stands at the zenith of modernity today might be passe tomorrow. As a budding prompt engineer, it's crucial to remain adaptable. Continual learning is not just a mantra; it's your lifeline. With each technological wave, be ready to surf, embrace its challenges, and evolve.

Rooted in Understanding:

Beyond the surface of each prompt lies an individual—a real person seeking information or connection. Keep their realities, emotions, and aspirations central to your creations. True empathy transcends being a mere attribute; it becomes the very pulse of effective prompt engineering. When genuine care intersects with design, the resulting prompts resonate deeper and truly serve.

Growth in Adversity:

In this evolving domain, setbacks are par for the course. Some prompts may falter, some models might not hit the right chord, and critiques could be hard-hitting. However, these are not dead-ends, but rather avenues for growth. Embrace these lessons; they are the crucibles in which sharper insights are forged.

Harness Collective Insight:

Though the work might sometimes feel solitary, prompt engineering thrives on collaboration. Engage with experts from varied fields, from linguistics to design, from ethics to user experience. This mosaic of perspectives will elevate your work, lending it nuances that a singular viewpoint might overlook.

Pushing Boundaries:

In the world of prompt engineering, you are more than a technician; you're a visionary. Every prompt becomes an opportunity, every interaction a potential revolution. Dare to venture beyond the familiar. Today's trailblazing concept could well be the standard of tomorrow.

Towards the Future:

As you stand at this juncture, ready to plunge into the depths of prompt engineering, maintain a forward-focused perspective. The potential is immense, its ramifications profound, and its role in shaping the future of tech-human dialogue undeniable. You're not just stepping into a job, but a movement—one that promises to redefine human-machine communication for the coming eras.

To the emerging prompt engineers, may these words act as a beacon. Amid the complex maze of coding, data, and algorithms, discover your distinctive tone. Recognize that you are part of a larger community, unified by a vision of creating meaningful, transformative interactions. Approach your journey with fervor, tenacity, and a clear sense of purpose. The digital realm eagerly awaits your groundbreaking endeavors.

www.ingramcontent.com/pod-product-compliance
Lightning Source LLC
LaVergne TN
LVHW051652050326
832903LV00032B/3764